THIS
RIGHTEOUS WAR

B. S. BARNES

RICHARD NETHERWOOD LIMITED

Acknowledgements

To the following people I owe a great debt of gratitude: without their help this study would have been the poorer.

John Major, University of Hull, for his encouragement, help and the long hours he spent correcting my work. Paul Reed, historian, for his unselfish sharing of his own work on this subject. Roderick Suddaby, Imperial War Museum, London, for allowing me to use the museum's archive.

All the staff of Hull's Local History Library, whose conscientious work and patience allowed my to unearth much from their own archive. The Departmental Officers (Archives), Ministry of Defence, Hayes, Middlesex. The Hull Daily Mail for featuring articles concerning my study, which led to the unearthing of much material. Radio Humberside, for allowing me air time to appeal for material. The staff of the Prince of Wales Own Museum, York, for allowing me to have access to the War Diaries of the East Yorkshire Regiment.

All the people of Humberside who gave or loaned diaries, letters, documents and photographs over the last three years.

To the people interviewed I owe a special debt of thanks, as without their very vivid memories this study would have been incomplete. They are: E. Land, G. Denis, E. Bancroft, F. Beeston, A. Barker and O. Weasenham, my grandmother.

Lastly, to Ann, who supported me for five years and enabled me to pursue an academic career. She spent many nights alone while I completed this study. To her I owe everything.

First Published by Richard Netherwood Limited
Fulstone Barn, New Mill, Huddersfield, England

Copyright © B. S. Barnes 1990

ISBN 1 872955 002

Designed by Andrew Ivett, Oxford
Typeset in Garamond by 'Word Up' Huddersfield
Printed in Yugoslavia by Gorenjski Tisk
Cover design by Station Graphics, Huddersfield
Published in Great Britain by Richard Netherwood Limited

Contents

Preface — John Prescott MP

It is an honour for me to write the preface to this instructive and illuminating book. Mr Barnes' love and admiration for his grandfather, Private Weasenham, shines through on every page. Above all, this study is an honourable epitaph for all the heroes, especially those of the Hull Pals Battalions, who fought in vain for a "land fit for heroes" in the "war to end all wars".

It is difficult for me to make an adequate contribution, as I am from a generation that has enjoyed nearly fifty years of peace in Europe. It is hard to appreciate the sacrifice and suffering, the pain and degradation and death of so many, that is graphically and horrifically illustrated in this work.

In future, when I stand on November 11 facing the War Memorial at Paragon Square in Hull, I will better understand, and even feel all the more, our homage to the dead, Thanks to Mr Barnes, the realities of battle and struggle at Oppy Wood and elsewhere will seem almost familiar. And I will think of Private Weasenham, alongside my own father, who lost his leg at Dunkirk in the Second World War. The misery of so many for so long was not rewarded with a better life. For four years, the sleepless nights, torn with fear and pain, wracked with illness and hunger, were endured often in depression, but also in good faith and Hull humour. Senior officers well behind the enemy lines, seldom felt the conditions of horror, or the bitter consequences of their own orders, ignored the growing list of casualties and enforced a barbaric discipline which saw the shooting of shell-shocked soldiers. Troops trained to fight a raw hand to hand combat that took only 0.03 per cent of the casualties in the First World War, were left to perish by their millions from anonymous bombs in the cold, damp, deathly, gas-choked trenches, which saw the first and often most brutal mass slaughter from the new military technology. Some French divisions revolted, and the Russians left the field to conduct their revolution; British soldiers fought on.

Yet there are many examples of unparalelled humanitarian generosity of spirit that can teach us all so much. In the lulls between artillery fire and bomb blasts, soldiers from the Hull Pals hurled tinned "Bully Beef" meat across the few yards between trenches in return for sausages from the German infantry. And to his dying day, Private Weasenham would not accept a critisism of his German counterparts. This moment of common solidarity between soldiers from warring nations, sharing the same degradation and horror of this war, is the shining hope of this book: that we can find a more civilised way of settling national differences.

Mr Barnes' book is an honour to his grandfather and to the Hull Pals, and a service to the memory of Hull and its people. It is not a glorification of war, but just a testimony to the soldiers who were often exploited but never unreliable. All were heroes, and we shall always remember them.

Dedication

This study is dedicated to the memory of my Grandfather who served as Pte. Robert Harris Weasenham, 11/682, 2nd Hull Service Battalion (Tradesman's), later to be the 11th Battalion, East Yorkshire Regiment. He joined at the Hull City Hall in September, 1914, trained in England and went to Egypt in December, 1915. In March, 1916, the Hull Units were sent to France to prepare for the Somme offensive.

He was badly wounded in the attack on Oppy Wood, 3rd May, 1917, and invalided out of the army.

Robert Harris Weasenham died in Hull Royal Infirmary, Anlaby Road, in 1968.

Still missed after all this time.

Foreword

AS A BOY I was raised on stories of my grandfather's exploits in the Great War. For hours he would sit and talk to me in the front room of 17/16th Avenue, North Hull Estate and I could not get enough. He died in 1968 and left no written record of his military service. In 1986 I decided to try and find out the details but all I had to go on were my own memories and what my grandmother could still recall. This information I sent to the Army Archives Office, who informed me they would try to trace his record but held out little hope. Many weeks later I received an answer telling me the search had been a success only because of his unusual surname of Weasenham. This basic outline of his service record was to launch me on a project that was to grow steadily and bring to the surface a period of Hull's history that existed in parts in various households in the city, much of it about to be thrown away. Bringing it together was to become an obsession and took over my life for three years.

I placed advertisements in the Hull Daily Mail and even went on Radio Humberside asking for information; the result was dozens of letters and telephone calls offering to loan or give diaries, letters, documents and photographs. It took two years hard work to copy and carefully file all of this material; it is now deposited in the Hull Local History Library where it will remain permanently.

My main working time was at night or in the early hours of the morning when my family was in bed and the house in darkness. My study desk would be lit by a small reading lamp as I worked, and I would slip into a silent subterreanean world populated by these forgotten people of so long ago. As I read their thoughts and pieced together the vast mosaic of their time it was like listening to the voices of ghosts. My thoughts were constantly occupied by my study and I dreamt of these long dead people frequently. My grandfather appeared to me in dreams, bathed in a radiant light, after which I would wake with a start and feel once again the warmth and security of his presence I knew so well as a child.

The surviving men from the Hull units gave long and most interesting interviews that have all been preserved on tape and are now in the archive; their names are as follows:

Gerald Denis.   King's Royal Rifle Corps., 21st battalion, 1915 to 1918. Still living in Hull.

Albert Barker.   4th Hull Pals, 13th Battalion, East Yorkshire Regiment, 1914 to 1918. Living in Cottingham.

Ernest Land.   2nd Hull Pals, 11th Battalion, East Yorkshire Regiment, 1914 to 1918. Living in Ellerker.

To them I owe a great debt as their very vivid memories gave substance to the written material left by their comrades.

This study is not in any way meant to be a glorification of war and all its attendant horrors. Nor is it an academic exercise: my aim has been to record, as well as I am able, the experience of these Hull units from the point of view of the ordinary soldier. These men deserve to be remembered, and if my three years' work sparks off some interest in Hull's part in the Great War then my work will not have been wasted.

"Let us rather raise a monument to the soldiers whose brave hearts only kept the ranks unbroken and met death — a monument to the faithful who were not famous, and who are precious as the continuity of the sunbeams is precious, though some of them fall unseen and on barrenness."

George Elliot - Felix Holt
(Quoted in Myriad Faces of War. Polity, 1986. p.353)

CHAPTER ONE

Hull, August, 1914

I N HULL and its surrounding areas there was a great bustle of activity in August, 1914, as reservists and Territorials joined their different units and moved out of the city:

> "I had no idea there were so many, in some houses at which I called two and three of the family, husbands and brothers, drawn out were by no means uncommon. These men are called out to fulfil Garrison duty." [1]

Even the local Music Halls were affected by the outbreak of hostitilies. The Three Aeros, trapeze artists, could not meet their engagements in Hull as they had been called up for military service.[2] The General Post Office was working as fast as it could sending out notices to thousands of reservists. On 3rd August many gathered in Posterngate and left by train the same evening.[3]

The people of Hull on 5th August were as yet unaware of the reality of the situation in Europe and most citizens prepared for war with an air of confidence. At this time Britain still ruled the waves and the Empire was world-wide; with such a glorious past the people of Hull met the declaration of war with Germany with a certainty that it would be a short-lived affair in which arrogant Germany would be taught a lesson. At local gatherings and at local theatres, speeches in support of the war were commonplace. On Monday, August 10th, there was a patriotic outburst at the Alexandra Theatre when portraits of high-ranking national figures were shown to the audience. A photograph of Admiral Jellicoe was shown to thunderous applause, and when one of the Kaiser was shown the band struck up with 'He'll have to get out and get under'. Lastly a picture of the King was shown and the audience rose as one and sang the National Anthem, whilst Territorials stood stiffly to attention. When the singing was over, cheer after cheer rang out for the King.[4]

In Hull rumours were rife of spies; sentries were under orders to shoot to kill if an individual tried to make off, when challenged. Some of the population were in a state of panic and ready to believe most stories:

> "Some foolish rumours among our own people of spies poisoning springs and water — I can see that it wants very little to put this population into

panic — a section of them believe anything." [5]

Troops came and went constantly and stories of troop movements became highly inventive:

> "A very curious and persistent rumour has been circulated in Hull, coming from numerous very reliable people, none of whom, however, have it at first hand, that bodies of Russian troops have landed in Scotland for the purpose of proceeding to Belgium." [6]

On Friday, 21st August, Thomas Pearson Taylor, aged 23 years, son of Alderman Taylor, was returning to Saltburn on his motor bike with his younger brother in the side-car when he was challenged by a sentry just before midnight. He either "did not heed or did not hear the repeated challenge" and was hit in the chest by a bullet, dying shortly after. The verdict was 'accidently shot'.

German residents in Hull were rounded up and kept aboard the Wilson liner Borodino in King George Dock:

> "Fully three hundred of our German residents have been arrested — the majority are reservists and several are well known in Hull, those on board are being well cared for and treated with every courtesy." [7]

Anti-German feeling never rose to hysteria in Hull in 1914 but it manifested itself in various ways. Shortly after the declaration of war a brick was hurled through the shop window of Mr. Charles Hohenrein, a naturalized Englishman, at 7 Waterworks Street. Victor Parker and Joseph Correl were seen running from the scene and arrested shortly after. Parker was seen to have thrown the brick and brought for trial to Hull Police Court. Parker went into the witness box and said he had been in Whitefriargate outside the newspaper offices when the declaration of war between England and Germany became known. Both he and his friend proceeded to the recruiting office in Pryme Street; he wished to join the Navy, his friend the Army. However, finding the office closed, the pair went to Waterworks Street and noticed a crowd had gathered outside Hohenrein's shop. Parker said he did not know Hohenrein was a naturalized Englishman and denied throwing the brick.

The Magistrate asked Parker: "Do you still intend to enlist?" He said he did. The Magistrate then said he could not condone what was alleged to have happened, though it might have been in the heat of the moment, but he did not want to prevent Parker from serving his country. The prisoner was committed for trial at the Quarter Sessions with bail of five pounds. [8]

All foreigners in Hull had to be registered with the authorities and any that did not found themselves on trial for being in breach of the 'alien restriction order'. The first case was a Mr. Charles Henry Spethmann, a German charged with failure to register. The first witness was a P.C. Dandy who stated he had visited the shop at 29 Witty Street where he saw the prisoner and a woman named Bertha K. Tommins. When asked about his nationality, Spethmann denied he was a German and Tommins claimed he was her husband and a Hull-born man. After questioning, Spethmann admitted he had lived in Hull only fourteen years and lied because he was afraid he would be sent to the ship. Charles Henry Tommins was charged with failing to notify the presence in his house of an alien. Bertha Tommins was charged with aiding and abetting the offence. Both she and Spethmann received six weeks' jail each and Mr. Tommins was fined ten pounds.

The chairman, Mr. Sharp, was not sure as to how he should deal with such a case, the like of which he had not heard before. He was reluctant to punish a woman and both the accused had unblemished characters. The police courts in Hull were full of such cases in August, 1914; judges were having to deal with a situation that was completely new to them and the rules guiding their judgements were, as yet, not at all clear.

Many magistrates were taking a lenient line with any man who, when brought for trial, declared his intention of joining up as soon as possible. A letter appeared in the Hull Daily Mail on August 24th from a Mr. H. E. C. Newham (Captain, National Reserve) showing concern about this practice; he felt that such men would discredit the King's uniform and such a situation would not be acceptable to men who had volunteered for a career as a regular.

The main local political organizations in 1914 were the Hull Liberal and Unionist (Conservative) Associations, of which both threw their weight behind the recruitment campaign and party politics were put aside. The infant Independent Labour Party, however, stood against a European war and told its members to resist any Governmental attempts to continue the present conflict:

> "The I.L.P. views with serious alarm the present European war. Brought about by secret alliances and understandings which in their origins have not been sanctified by the people themselves.
>
> We stand by the efforts of the international working class movement to unite the workers of the nations concerned in the great effort to prevent their Governments from entering upon war." [9]

The Labour movement, however, was not strong enough to resist the rise of nationalist feeling in the city and throughout the country. Their warnings were lost amid the bustle as the city prepared for war.

Letters from the front were now being received in Hull and painted a picture of troops eager to come to grips with the enemy. Pte. P. O'Brian wrote:

> "I have never seen such enthusiasm, old men, women and children fight in the street to get close enough to shake hands, or beg a piece of cloth or a button from our uniforms — at one village women clamoured for locks of hair from us, even the sick are brought to the doors to see us pass." [10]

The British Expeditionary Force had not yet made contact with the enemy and there was no way anyone could know that the French had been defeated in battle at Morhange-Sarrebourg with very heavy losses on the same day this letter was published.

At least one person in Hull was not prepared to accept all he was told. Mr. J. Claytor of Campbell Street wrote to the Hull Daily Mail:

"Sir, Is it not remarkable that nearly all the reports of the war are unfavourable to the opponents of Great Britain? Many accounts are to hand of brutal acts committed by Germany and Austria. If we believed all the narratives we read we would be inclined to think that British and Belgian soldiers were invincible in war and innocent of any brutality whatever, but such is not the case. I would advise my fellow workers not to be beguiled by reports we are getting at present." [11]

Letters from relatives and friends still in Europe continued to arrive in Hull with tales of German barbarity. Mrs. Olsen of 6 Kingston Gardens, Hull, received a letter from a Belgian lady, Madame Yohanson, 8 Vingerling Street, Antwerp. The letter mentions the Germans at Brussels threatening the farmers and burning down whole villages, and states that Antwerp is in a state of panic not knowing if the Germans will move against them. Germans living in Antwerp were driven out of the country and their houses pelted with stones, while pianos and other articles were dragged into the streets and smashed up. Many left without a penny: a gentleman who was staying with Madame Yohanson, who had been a sailor in Belgian ships for 40 years and receiving a pension, left quickly for Rotterdam where Madame Yohanson took him some belongings. Women married to Germans were forced to leave, the people of Antwerp were raging mad at the reports of German activities around Brussels and marched German civilians through the streets, before they left in thousands. The Germans are reported to have ordered civilians to eat grass and, if they would not, they were forced to eat it.

Only soldiers' letters that gave a rosy picture of the events in Europe were printed; no other kind could get through the censor's screen. Later in August the British troops were so hard pressed that they had no time to write home and for quite some time the public were kept in the dark, until matters became so grave they could be concealed no longer.

In Hull preparations were under way to cater for the expected casualties. A meeting was held at the Hull Guildhall under the supervision of the Red Cross Society with the purpose of forming a committee to equip temporary hospitals. This was attended by one hundred of Hull's leading citizens, mostly female, and Lady Nunburnholme took the chair in the absence of her husband. The meeting endorsed the feeling among the political parties that all party political considerations must be set aside to help the country through its present crisis.

The offer of premises to be used as hospitals had been received from various quarters in the City. Messrs. Reckitts offered to donate their social hall and other halls on their premises for conversion. In central Hull promises of accommodation were obtained at the Metropole, the Waltham Street Schoolroom, the Baptist Schoolroom in Trafalgar Street and another in Quay Street. In West Hull four schoolrooms were offered.

At this time there were already in existence nine Voluntary Aid Detachments. Col. Milburn asked for volunteers to take over the equipping and management of the new hospitals. A central store was to be set up that could be drawn on, with the central administration office in Peel Street. The provision of the nursing and transport staff was to be the responsibility of the Territorial Authorities and St. John's Ambulance Brigade. By August 6th one hundred volunteers had offered their help. In the months to come the hospitals in Hull, temporary or not, would have their services stretched to the limit when the full impact of the war hit the city.

NOTES

1. Thorpe, G. Diaries. August 4th, 1914.
2. Hull Daily Mail. August 4th, 1914.
3. Ibid.
4. Ibid. August 10th, 1914.
5. Thorpe, G. Diaries. August 26th, 1914.
6. Ibid. August 30th, 1914.
7. Ibid. August 1st, 1914.
8. Hull Daily Mail. August 5th, 1914.
9. The Dawn. Volume II. No. 17. August, 1914. p.2. (Labour publication. Hull Local History Library).
10. Hull Daily Mail. August 20th, 1914.
11. Ibid.

CHAPTER TWO

Reporting the War
August/September, 1914

O N AUGUST 5th, 1914, the advance guard of the German army had reached the Belgian forts at Liège and had been checked by the Belium forces who put up a brave resistance; this initial success misled Allied Intelligence as to the weight of the German columns. Shortly afterwards the German heavy howitzers caught up with the spearhead and pummelled the line of forts at Liège into submission and cleared the way for the main body. [1]

These events were reported with relish in the Hull Daily Mail, and the holding up of the German advance guard was seen as a major victory. But by the time this news was reported the German columns had already begun their advance towards the Franco-Belgian Border.

The French at this time had a policy of attack being the best form of defence and favoured the bayonet charge above all else, but the latest machine guns made them pay dearly for such tactics. Liège was reported as a fiasco for the enemy and massive losses, some 25,000 men, were supposedly suffered by the German army, though in the same issue of the Hull Daily Mail appeared a small item on the front page: "Germans 13 miles from Brussels."

This form of blatant propaganda was kept up by the Hull Daily Mail until the situation got so bad the truth could no longer be kept from the public, and this had a direct influence on recruiting in the city.

French troops did advance in Alsace, but because of serious reverses elsewhere where forced to call off their sortie towards Metz. The forts at Liège held up the German armies for only a short time, after which the entire line of Belgian forts was reduced. The first news that Liège had been evacuated came on August 19th, when the Hull Daily Mail remonstrated with the population for putting the worst possible interpretation on the news that the Belgian Government had moved from Brussels to Antwerp. The reason given for this was that Brussels was an unfortified city with many historic buildings and the Authorities did not wish to see it destroyed by shelling.

> "These innocent pessimists shake their heads. They say we may be fighting brilliant little engagements but the Germans keep forging ahead. Nothing could be more erroneous than this view." [2]

This view was, of course, correct and apart from minor hold-ups the Schlief-fen Plan [3] was running on time and the field-grey columns were sweeping all from their path. The news being fed to the city of Hull, however, would have none of it and argued that it was all part of the Allies' plan now that the British Expeditionary Force had taken the field:

"The Allies might be allowed to have a plan as well as the Germans." [4]

The German Imperial Forces were not marching in a straight line but in a great curve, with the purpose of encircling Paris and so outflanking the Allies. The Belgian army had fought well at Liège and could, had it so desired, have held the Germans up even longer by giving battle. However, the decision to withdraw to Antwerp was seen as a masterly stroke: there it would be a threat to the German flank and would live to fight again later in the War. [5]

As the Germans advanced, their policy of dealing with the civilian popula-tion was harsh and many reports were filtering back to Hull of atrocities committed by the victorious German forces:

"Horrors of the War
Kaiser's Troops Leave Track of Ruin."

"According to the report of the Prefect of Badonviller 78 houses were burn-ed with petrol, the Germans have taken 15 hostages. At Bremenell an old man and woman, aged 74 years, have been burned in their house. Letters found on German soldiers who have been killed or wounded plainly demonstrate that these atrocities have been committed to the orders of the Commanding Officers. Germans have set fire to villages as a general measure and also killed the inhabitants and these atrocities have been com-mitted in areas defended by the French Army and not by civilians." [6]

The details of these allegations can never be substantiated but it is a fact that whole towns, Louvain for instance, were sacked and burned to the ground and hundreds of men, women and children were executed in reprisals against acts of hostility against the German Forces. This was a deliberate act by the military to terrorize the civilian population into a passive role; it was in general successful and was to remain official German Army policy until 1945. The German high command made no secret of the way they subdued the civilian populations of captured territories.

On the 21st August, and after so many statements to the contrary, the unthinkable happened:

"The German forces entered Brussels. The boom of cannon and the sound of martial music filled the air. On they came, preceded by a scouting party of Uhlans (Cavalry), infantry, horse artillery and sappers with a complete siege train." [7] A special feature of the triumphal entry was a line of 100 motor cars on which were mounted machine guns. Each regiment and battery was headed by its own band. Then came the fifes and drums and the soldiers' continuous singing of 'Deutchland über Alles'. The troops marched briskly to the great square and, upon the command of a whistle, broke into the goose step as the people of Brussels watched in awe. Hour after hour the troops marched through Brussels, "some of the regiments presented a very fine sight, the troops were in fine fettle and greatly impressed the citizens." [8]

After the bad news from Brussels, the Germans reached Namur and laid seige to the fortress; once again the heavy artillery came into its own and began to pour in a deadly fire of high explosive. The headlines of the Hull papers concentrated on the war in the east, of the steamroller advance of the Russian army and of defeats inflicted on Austria by Serbia. But on the same day these bulletins were printed the French suffered defeats with heavy losses in the Ardennes: their troops attacked with the bayonet and were mown down in droves by carefully sited machine guns. [9] This news was, unsurprisingly, not revealed at the time.

The late war news on Monday, 24th August, told of Germany's treacherous use of the white flag, a story first published in an Antwerp paper. According to the report, a Belgian Commandant was about to accept a German surrender when he was shot dead. No date or places are given and considering the whole Belgian army was on the retreat it seems strange that any Germans would show a white flag. The story goes on to relate how prisoners and wounded were ill-treated or killed by German troops. This part does not sound so incredible. [10]

Meanwhile in Belgium the Germans had crushed the last of the great line of fortresses at Namur and had continued their advance. On August 23rd they blundered into the British at Mons and launched two army-corps against two British divisions. The British rifle fire was so fierce that the Germans reported large numbers of machine guns in the British ranks. The battle at Mons was a small encounter by later standards but it was the first British battle of the Great War. Later the legend of the Angel of Mons grew; she is said to have appeared to warn the English troops of a trap and so they escaped. In fact the French on the right of the B.E.F. had fallen back and so the English had to start a fighting retreat in hot humid weather. [11]

The headlines in Hull on August 25th read:

"Allied Retreat on the French Frontier". [12]

No mention was made of the fight being at Mons but the battle was described in detail:

> "The retirements explained — An official French communiqué concerning the situation in Belgium states that, to the west of the Meuse the British army was attacked by the Germans and under fire the British resisted with admirable imperturbability. The French army carried away by their élan, were received by a murderous fire. They did not yield but a counter attack by the Prussian Guard compelled them to fall back." [13]

More details of the fighting in France were being reported on Thursday, 27th August, especially the B.E.F.'s stand at Mons. "Dogged does it", said the headline. The story itself was given by men on the spot and stated the facts of the matter truthfully. The Prussian soldiers are reported to have fought with a bravery and complete disregard for life that was magnificent. Wave after wave was sent against the much smaller British force that resisted every shock with discipline and marksmanship that was feared by the Germans and marvelled at by the French. [14]

Captain Walter Bloem was with the Brandenberg Grenadiers and had been revelling in the success of the German forces as they advanced to Mons. He looked forward to teaching the British a lesson, but after the first engagement Bloem was forced to change his opinion of the British as his proud regiment was reduced to no more than company strength:

> "Wherever I looked, right or left were dead and wounded, quivering in convulsions, groaning terribly, blood oozing from fresh wounds. They apparently knew something about war, these cursed English." [15]

Mounds of dead covered the battlefield and according to the Hull Daily Mail the British troops had to be restrained from following up their success in holding off the Germans. When Gen. Joffre decided to order a general withdrawal there was almost a mutiny among the British soldiers. But when the time came, the British troops made an orderly withdrawal from Mons; they had fought, inflicted enormous losses and melted away intact as a fighting force. What the B.E.F. lacked in numbers they more than made up for in quality.

On the 28th August the Hull Daily Mail headlines were full of bad news:

> "A further retreat by the Allied army.
> Another retirement.
> Forced Back."

A leading article said a terrific German onslaught was now in progress and although it was hoped the advance of the enemy could be stayed, the situation did not warrant too much optimism at this stage. Now that Alsace was abandoned, French troops were pouring northward to stem the German advance from Belgium. It was hoped these new dispositions would help, but Englishmen and Frenchmen:

> "must face coolly the chance that the Germans will be able to press home their attack."

Precautions were now well under way for the defence of Paris and the Military Governor of that ancient city had prepared for all eventualities:

> "Such too is the spirit in which Great Britain has entered upon this righteous war." [16]

On the 26th August the B.E.F. made another stand at the little town of Le-Cateau, giving the 2nd Corps time to withdraw, then continued the retreat. The battles at Mons and Le-Cateau were small affairs compared to later battles and they certainly only checked briefly the advancing German Army but, for the first time since Waterloo, British blood had been shed in Europe and I think it is no coincidene that the numbers of young men recruited in Hull rose sharply in September, 1914.

The German Army Commanders now abandoned their original plan and, thinking the B.E.F. broken, wheeled before Paris and exposed their right flank to the Allies. The French attacked the Germans on both flanks of the B.E.F., who had now stopped their retreat. The B.E.F. turned and began a cautious advance into the gap between two German Armies. So began the 'Battle of the Marne.' The German position was now far too exposed for their liking and on 9th September they began to retreat. The B.E.F. was still advancing into the gap between the German Armies, finding no opposition and moving at a rate of eight miles per day as compared with their thirty miles per day in the retreat. But the men were worn out and their ranks badly depleted: the officers of the B.E.F. moved their troops forward with great caution into an unexpected vacuum. The French attacks on either side of the B.E.F. were held by the Germans, but they could not defend their rear areas and so pulled back.

On the 14th September the exhausted German Army reached the Aisne where they were joined by fresh troops released by the fall of Maubeuge. Here they dug holes in the ground, set up machine guns and waited. The Allied advance hesitated and stopped: the campaign from the Marne was over. Trench warfare had begun.

As 1914 drew to a close the warring armies faced each other exhausted. The Belgian army was nearly destroyed and all but a small part of their country was under German occupation. The large French professional army, which had fought with more courage than skill, was badly mauled. The Germans, because of their inability to gain a decisive victory, stood at bay, unsure of what to do next. Russia, in August, had come in with the Allies and Germany now faced a war on two fronts.

The B.E.F., a relatively small force compared to other armies, had played its part in all of this. Actions at Mons, Le-Cateau and the Marne had shown the quality of its men and leaders. The Germans were made to respect this small regular army and the Kaiser's remark of them being 'Contemptible' had been proved to be untrue. In the final desperate fighting of 1914, as the armies tried to outflank each other, they had helped defend the town of Ypres (in an engagement later known as 'First Ypres'). By the end of the year British casualties had reached 86,000. In April 1915 the Germans renewed their attacks at Ypres ('Second Ypres') and again the B.E.F. played its part in one of the fiercest battles of the war. After the two battles for Ypres the old regular army virtually ceased to exist; reinforcements were needed badly, and the stage was now set for Kitchener's men to make their entrance into a type of warfare never seen before.

NOTES

1. Hart, B. L. History of the First World War. (Cassel, 1970) p.49.
2. Hull Daily Mail. August 19th, 1914.
3. Schlieffen Plan. See Appendix III.
4. Hull Daily Mail. August 19th, 1914.
5. Hart, B. L. The History of the First World War. (Cassel, 1970) p.52.
6. Hull Daily Mail. August 19th, 1914.
7. Hull Daily Mail. August 21st, 1914.
8. Ibid. August 22nd, 1914.
9. Sheffield, D. G. A Pictorial History of World War One. (Bison Books, 1982) p.24.
10. Hull Daily Mail. August 24th, 1914.
11. Taylor, A. J. P. The First World War. (Penguin, 1987) p.29.
12. Hull Daily Mail. August 25th, 1914.
13. Ibid.
14. Ibid. August 27th, 1914.
15. Babington, A. For the Sake of Example. (Leo Cooper, 1984) p.4.
16. Hull Daily Mail. August 28th, 1914.

CHAPTER THREE

'This Righteous War'
Raising the 'Hull Pals'

O N THURSDAY, 14th MARCH, 1914, great excitement was generated in Hull in expectation of a visit by the first Battalion East Yorkshire Regiment. The troops detrained on Thursday morning and assembled in Paragon Station yard. The picture that presented itself to the public at noon must have been an impressive sight as the Battalion stood formed in quarter column facing the Mayor, the Sherriff, most of Hull's leading citizens, Territorial officers, veterans, reservists and other privileged visitors. Great crowds had by now gathered at the iron gates on the Anlaby Road side and at the Station Hotel side to watch the scarlet-clad troops march out. On roof tops and on every balcony spectators awaited their appearance and on buildings within the immediate vicinity flew flags and bunting. The Hull Times describes the scene:

> "Here was a spectacle to stir the martial spirit of onlookers, who were not accustomed to the rattle of musketry and steel and the smart precision of regular soldiers." [1]

The Battalion stood in review order with Col. Benson at its head, and behind him seventeen officers and three hundred and fifty men. The King's colours and Regimental colours were in the centre with the customary colour party of two officers, colour sergeants and privates with fixed bayonets forming the escort. Col. Benson barked his orders at the solid square of red and the whole Battalion fixed bayonets with a simultaneous click and gave the general salute with the band playing. With the men stood squarely at attention the Mayor, wearing his chain of office, gave an address of welcome.

At the Artillery Barracks in Park Street a large crowd had formed in anticipation of a reception being held there by Lord Nunburnholme, the Lord Lieutenant of the East Riding. His Lordship arrived dressed in the full uniform of Lord Lieutenant, as befitted such an important occasion, and as the central figure acted as the Chairman of the Reception Committee. The Mayor's party arrived at the Park Street drill hall ahead of the 1st Battalion, known as the "Snappers", [2] and included the Mayor and Mayoress, Miss Hargreaves the Sheriff, Mrs. Ohlson and Mrs. Asprey. The red-clad troops marched smartly over Park Street bridge to a rousing welcome from the waiting populace. As they approached, the doors of the drill hall were thrown open and Col. Benson [3] and his Battalion, fully equipped in their bright uniforms and pickelhaube helmets, wheeled smartly into the Barracks and halted. The Colonel ordered his troops, "Officers and colours, take your post in review order". The band struck up the National Anthem and the colours moved to the front facing Col. Benson, the King's colours and Regimental colours in a line with the officers.

Lord Nunburnholme addressed the gathering and reminded those present that the last time the Regiment had visited the city was in 1822. Following the reception Lord Nunburnholme entertained a number of officers and friends to luncheon in the officers' mess at the Barracks. The party toasted His Majesty the King and Col. Benson and his officers. The sumptuous luncheon was provided by Mr. Colomb of the Station Hotel. Once their dinner was over the Battalion left the Artillery Barracks and embarked on a route march through the City streets. The route took them via Spring Bank, Prince's Avenue, Pearson Park, Beverley Road, Prospect Street, the City Square, Porter Street, Anlaby Road, to the Hull City Football Ground where they were entertained by a match. As the scarlet-clad troops marched smartly into the City Square, flags fluttered in the breeze from all the major buildings. Several hundred people had been waiting for over an hour to see the visitors and numbers of the North Eastern Railway Company's staff were watching the scene from the roof of the Dock Offices. Mr. G. Morley, the Chief Constable, kept the route clear for the troops and marshalled operations in the City Centre. It was a glorious sunny day as the Drum and Fife Band played the 'Snappers' through the streets and as the colours came into view, hats were raised on all sides. To obtain a better view many spectators boarded standing tramway cars:

> "One man pushed a handcart to the edge of the crowd and mounted it, thus getting a splendid view. The visitors are capital marchers and they very quickly passed through the square and on to Carr Lane and Anlaby Road. The drum and fife band were very favourably spoken of." [4]

From Porter Street, along Hessle Road up to the Boulevard, the route was lined with thousands of women and children. There were comparatively few men in the crowd but even so it was much larger than expected. In the small playground at the front of St. James's School, Porter Street, the teachers had assembled their pupils in line, each one carrying a paper flag on a wooden stick. As the soldiers marched past, the children waved their flags and saluted.

Large numbers of police were needed to control the crowds and the tramway service was held up in parts, but those on the tops of the cars were given an excellent view of events. On St. James's Street corner one woman was overcome by the heat and excitement and collapsed in a fit; she was taken into a shop by a constable and others. Hawkers did very good business, especially among the children. Five thousand spectators attended the football match at the end of the march and the Hull side won by five goals to one.

In the evening the Sheriff entertained the officers to dinner. Later the Battalion were the guests at a Smoking Concert at the Hull City Hall which was attended by the Mayor and Sheriff of Hull. Thousands of spectators filled the City Square outside and cheered off the troops in their scarlet tunics as they marched off to Paragon Station, just before 11pm:

> "It is many years since Hull was the scene of so much military enthusiasm." [4]

At this time the sight of troops was still a rarity and a cause for great excitement among the population of Hull. Little could they know of the conflict that lay ahead of them in the coming months. Soon the marching troops of the Snappers would have changed their gay scarlet for a khaki battle-dress and many of them would not live to see the Summer of 1915. The events that were to overtake the country had not yet become apparent to folk concerned only with making a living and getting by, but soon they would demand attention and in the next four years Hull would have its fill of military uniforms and the sounds of marching men as the City was plunged into a war, the likes of which has never been seen before or since.

By the end of July, 1914, people were aware of the situation in Europe and some watched events with great trepidation. One such individual was Mr. George Thorpe who was 67 years of age in 1914. Mr. Thorpe kept a detailed diary, completing one volume per year from 1911 to 1939. The volumes from the Great War period give us a glimpse of the mood of the City during the war years:

> "Affairs are so gloomy on the Continent — at this moment it seems that the black outlook will involve such a fearful catastrophe that future historians will record it in crimson, to represent the awful bloodshed it at present seems impossible to avert." [5]

Prophetic words at a time when most people did not believe England would be dragged into a European war, even though reservists were being called up and docks and power stations were guarded by troops in Hull in early 1914.

Gerald Denis, then a young man living in Hull said:

> "We thought it would be over by Christmas, there was no feel of urgency." [6]

The crisis on the Continent seemed so remote that few thought it would produce such a chain reaction, as George Thorpe wrote:

> "There is a strong peace party in England and we are bound to no nation by treaties either for offence or defence and have no interest, direct or indirect in the dispute in the East of Europe." [7]

The Hull Daily Mail carried large recruiting advertisements:

> "Your King and Country need you. Will you answer your Country's call?

Each day is fraught with the gravest possibilities, and at this very moment the Empire is on the brink of the greatest war in the history of the world." [8]

Men joined the colours from all walks of life and recruiting carried on steadily as troops came into the City and left for unknown destinations.

On the night of the 4th August and the morning of the 5th, the 5th (Cyclist) Battalion, East Yorkshire Regiment, assembled in Corporation Field, Park Street, for a medical examination. Afterwards the men continued their preparations and commandeered cycles and motor vehicles, as they were allowed to do under martial law. The Cyclists left in detachments later that day. [8]

By the 15th August recruiting in Hull had slowed to a trickle and in the <u>Hull Daily Mail</u> the headlines carried an appeal from Lord Kitchener for 100,000 men to enlist to form a new army. No men would be refused who were physically fit for active service and between the ages of 19 and 30 years. Old soldiers up to 42 years and ex-regular non-commissioned officers were wanted to train the new volunteer army. Men who enlisted under these conditions were to be released the minute the war ended, "whether this lasts three weeks or three years, should the war last over three years their continuance of service will be optional." [9] It was frequently stated that Lord Kitchener's new army was to be trained as a regular unit for home defence. This was incorrect as they were to be used when and where they were needed, be it home or abroad. [9]

Lord Nunburnholme called a meeting to be held at the Hull City Hall at 12 noon on 21st August, to be attended by many of Hull's most prominent citizens, with the purpose of furthering the movement for obtaining recruits for the second army.

There had been a slight improvement in recruiting by the 25th with 50 local men enlisting at Pryme Street, Wenlock Barracks and at East Hull Barracks. Since the war began approximately 500 Hull men had joined up, but these had mainly been reservists (old soldiers) who joined for a year. What was wanted was the young men between 18 and 25 in the regular service for the duration of the war. [10] Apart from the first flourish after the declaration of war the young men of Hull did not come forward in any great numbers in August, 1914. The main reason for the slowness in recruiting was thought to be the poor position and drabness of the Hull recruiting offices. There was also thought to be insufficient staff on hand, especially at Pryme Street, to deal with all enquiries. It was proposed a large tent be set up in the City, but the Lord Mayor disagreed saying "enthusiasm would be roused when it was really realized that the country is in danger". The reports of German defeats had lulled the population into a false sense of security. Mr. J. R. Bell, the well-known local Labour leader, said he was confident they would get the men they required in this district if they would employ some of the Colour Sergeants and Sergeant Majors of the Volunteer Corps to appeal directly to the men. [10]

The response in Hull to Lord Kitchener's appeal was not at all satisfactory and many irate letters appeared in the <u>Hull Daily Mail</u> accusing the citizens of apathy, laziness and even cowardice:

> "Now, now, now is the time! To arms, to arms, or it will be forever too late. Your King and Country wants you. Your fathers and mothers want you (if they are not lily-livered) to at once prepare to acquit yourselves like men — for the day of reckoning is at hand."
>
> R. Henderson,
> Sculcoates Lane, Hull. [10]

It was proposed in more than one letter published that if the young men of Hull would not go of their own accord, a Bill should be passed in Parliament making them go and if this was not possible local employers should not employ anyone between the age of 20 and 30. This idea of compulsory military service was revolutionary in a country with a volunteer army and it was not to be taken up by the Government until 1916, when the wasteage in life far outstripped recruitment.

The tone of letters in the <u>Hull Daily Mail</u> became hysterically jingoistic, most of them being written by people living in affluent middle class areas or by people too old to go to war:

> "Come lads, show a leg, don't let Liverpool have all the say, what if they have got 1,000 in a week. Hull should get as many in a day."
>
> One of the too olds,
> National Reserve. [10]

On Saturday afternoon, 22nd August, a large number of National Reservists had been inspected by Lord Nunburnholme on Corporation Fields. Capt. W. M. Carver commanded the men. The Lord Lieutenant was accompanied by Col. A. Lambert-White, V.D., the Vice-Chairman of the Territorial Association. Giving a short address Lord Nunburnholme expressed his appreciation of the patriotism of the men and remarked how they were setting an example to the younger men of the city:

> "In this way we are fighting on the side of freedom and we had to meet the strongest military organization that had ever existed." [10]

His Lordship could not have known that this organization was to rout the B.E.F. at Mons the next day as it continued on its course through France. Two hundred men from the National Reserve had already gone to supplement the regular units and more would be required soon, but some would be called upon for civil duties.

In an obvious reference to the poor recruiting in Hull, Col. White told the gathering he was confident the men of the reserve would do credit not only to Hull but to the Empire if they were called upon to go abroad. The older men were setting an example to the young men of Hull. They wanted to see more of the young manhood of the city coming forward to serve in His

Majesty's army, and he suggested they should use their influence to that end. He hoped the young men of Hull would not be lacking in patriotism or courage. [10].

The local papers in Hull pressed for more recruits as the situation in France grew worse and the remnants of the British and French continued their retreat. Censorship had been imposed on English papers since the 2nd August, [11] and so the people of Hull had little knowledge of the serious state of affairs that faced the B.E.F. as it made a second desperate stand at the little French town of Le-Cateau on the 26th August. The citizens of Hull reading such headlines as 'Russians occupy East Prussia', 'Malines recaptured', 'Greatest danger is past', [12] can have seen little to be concerned about and this is reflected in the poor response to recruiting in the City in late August.

In the Hull Daily Mail a stirring Edgar Marsh cartoon depicted Britannia appealing to the sons of the Empire to join up:

> "To arms, your country needs you, Britain even yet hardly understands the gravity of the situation. We shall need at least 500,000 men on the continent before we have finished. You will have to fight. Recruiting in Hull has been slow. We appeal to able bodied young men to be up and doing. It is better to volunteer like gentlemen that to be taken by a sort of military press-gang in six months' time." [12]

This is the first official hint at conscription, and a sure sign of the concern felt by the country's leaders as the situation in France deteriorated.

Numerous letters continued to be published in the Hull Daily Mail concerning recruiting:

> "Sir, Are we patriotic in Hull? Whether we are or not, the fact remains that recruiting for the army, so far as Hull is concerned, is very poor. I cannot think that the shocking response to Lord Kitchener's appeal is due to either indifference or to cowardice. There must be a reason why young men are holding back. A friend of mine, a few days ago, expressed his intention of enlisting, he now states he will not do so unless more of his own class volunteer.
>
> What my friend is suggesting is this: that instead of some of the larger employers of labour in Hull giving big donations of money they should use their influence to organize Corps of the middle class young men — clerks, tailors, drapers assistants, grocers assistants, warehousemen and artisans. Then we should see men living, sleeping and training in company of others of their own class.
>
> It is the idea of having to herd with all types of men now being enlisted that keeps our young athletes and men of good birth and training from joining the colours. At least that is the opinion I have gathered from conversation with likely candidates — I am Sir, etc."

Middle Class.
Newland. August 26th, 1914.

The idea of units being raised along class lines shows how firmly the whole concept of social class was implanted into the consciousness of the people of Hull. The introduction of class-based battalions was, as we shall see later, to be the catalyst that sparked off the forming of Hull's Service Battalions.

The recruiting offices themselves came in for much criticism, especially Pryme Street, as it was felt that not enough effort was being put into the recruiting drive by the civil and military authorities in Hull:

> "Sir, One of your correspondents in tonight's Mail recommends tents as special recruiting centres being rigged up in various parts of the city, to attract young men to enlist.
>
> This seems a far more likely way to get hold of suitable men that the present arrangements, viz, to have to present themselves at Pryme Street. A fortnight ago the case of two young men was brought to my notice. They went to the Pryme Street recruiting office with the intention of enlisting. After waiting some time they left without being interviewed, solely because there was a stream of others before their turn. Next day their ardour had somewhat cooled and the result is they have not been to Pryme Street again.
>
> No! Sir, many of us feel sure if the enlisting could take place under more attractive circumstances, such, for instance, as a tent displaying the Union Jack, with a call for volunteers, numbers would come forward to the aid of their country who as yet hesitate to apply at the more formidable and gloomy recruiting office in our city. Make the recruiting offices bright and attractive and there will be no lack of volunteers. I am Sir, etc.''
>
> Pro Bono Angleterre. August 25th, 1914.

The Editor of the Hull Daily Mail received other letters on the lack of patriotism in Hull but these were not published because of the better recruiting figures for the 24th and 25th August. [12]

At Wenlock Barracks on Anlaby Road another recruiting office was opened on the 25th August by Col. George Easton, and in the Hull Daily Mail on the 27th the 4th Battalion East Yorkshire Regiment advertised for men under forty to enlist for foreign service at Londesborough Street Barracks between 9 a.m. and 9 p.m. on Friday, 28th August.

One letter entitled "Women and local recruiting" scolded the young men of Hull for not stepping forward, and asked what women in Hull could do to stir them out of their lethargy in this time of need:

> "Up up you men, single men of Hull,
> Hark to your country's call,
> Your country has urgent need of you,
> Immediate need for all.
> To your shame never let it be said,
> you waited for press gang's force.
> You know the old adage truly says,
> There's nowt like a willing horse.
>
> Here is just the chance to show your grit,
> Loose sweethearts clinging arms,
> If single, able bodied and fit,
> Smooth mother's fond alarms,

Give ready service and volunteer.
We'll send you off with a ringing cheer,
Better a hero in a battlefield dead,
Than a smug live coward safe in bed.

Shirley Hills,
Tower Hill,
Hessle. [13]

Things were very gloomy in the City of Hull on Friday, 28th August [14] as the realization of the true situation was forced upon the consciousness of the citizens. Britain was now totally committed to the war in Europe and soon the men of Hull would be needed in great numbers. The recruiting authorities were now becoming more organized and offices were in operation in various parts of the city; the advertisement by the 4th Battalion, East Yorkshire Regiment had been a success and 640 men had volunteered for service overseas.

One of these young men was Cyril Hebb of 13 Edwards Avenue, Buckingham Street, Holderness Road. In a letter to his mother in August he asked for her permission to volunteer for service abroad. The letter was written after a

Cyril Hebb served in the 1/4th East Yorks, 1914-1919. On the left we see the fresh young boy who wrote to his mother in 1914, asking for permission to serve overseas. On the right we see a man hardened by four years of war. Cyril Hebb died of influenza in 1919 and is buried in Hedon Road Cemetery, Hull

gathering was addressed by Col. Shaw who said he saw no reason why single men should stay at home and that those who did not volunteer were half-hearted lads. Cyril pointed out to his mother that "if we could get more men into France it would be a short war and that it was very likely they would see no fighting." Cyril joined the 1/4th East Yorkshire Regiment as Pte. 1885 and saw some of the fiercest fighting in the front line, only to die of influenza in 1919 at the age of 23 years. [15]

Lord Nunburnholme wrote to the Editor of the Hull Daily Mail and proposed the raising of a Hull Commercial Battalion. This idea had been raised already earlier in August and would involve men such as clerks and others engaged in commercial business who would wish to serve their King and Country by enlisting. In this way they would be sure of serving with their friends and would not be put into Battalions with complete strangers. The formation of such a Hull Battalion had already been sanctioned by Lord Kitchener. [16]

The conditions of service would be the same as in other Battalions of the regular army. The new Battalion would be 1,000 strong and known as the 7th (Hull) Battalion, East Yorkshire Regiment (later the 10th Battalion, nick-named the Hull Commercials). Men wishing to enlist would have to go to Wenlock Barracks and recruiting would begin from 10 a.m. on Tuesday, 1st September. For the present recruits joining would be billeted in their own homes. Ex-officers were asked to help with training until others were appointed to the battalion and Major W. H. Carver was temporarily appointed Acting Adjutant. [16]

As the month of September opened the recruiting drive for the new Commercial Battalion began with enthusiastic meetings at Ripon Hall, Holderness Road. By the 2nd September 100 men had joined from Reckitts and many more from other firms in Hull. New recruiting offices were opened at 217 Holderness Road on Friday, 4th September.

Reginald Pearson, a merchant seaman, arrived in Hull during the recruiting drive for the Hull Commercials to find the city in a state of excitement. As most of his friends had joined up he decided he too would enlist in this exclusive Hull unit, only to be rejected on the grounds that his present work was of great importance to the war effort, and so he put to sea once more. In January, 1915, he again returned to Hull and was paid off for a week's holiday; taking the opportunity of being temporarily unemployed he presented himself at the Hull City Hall:

"And to my joy was this time accepted, and better still, posted to the Commercials, joining my pals once more." [17]

Though the recruiting figures were improving at the start of September, the articles and letters in the Hull Daily Mail reached fever pitch as they heaped abuse on the young men of Hull:

"Petticoats supplied free, to all the young men of Hull who are afraid to

Men from Reckitt's factory enlist, 1914. In the back row, second from right, is Robert Henry West, who was to be one of a firing party that executed a Hull man in 1917

Enlisting men for the Commercials. Wenlock Barracks, September 1914

enlist." [18]

Much criticism was voiced concerning sporting fixtures, as it was considered a luxury that could be dispensed with at such a time of national danger. Many young men who were fit enough to play on the sportsfield were looked upon as fodder for the recruiting sergeant:

> "Pray teach our gallant athletes all,
> All can't have craven souls,
> To go and shoot the Germans first,
> And then go shooting goals."
>
> A.T. [19]

The Rugby Football Union cancelled all International fixtures and County Championship matches for the season, urging all clubs to do the same with league fixtures. The union urged all players to enlist immediately. [20]

By 7th September the recruiting offices in Hull were at last getting men in considerable numbers; by the 8th September the clerks and white collar workers of Hull had formed the 1,000 men needed for the Commercial Battalion. The men still lived at home and for the time being drilled on Walton Street fairground without arms and without uniforms, an arm band being their only identification. As the new Battalions were organized the recruiting offices in all parts of Hull were opened from 8 a.m. until midnight, such was the response to the new class based units.

Jingoistic letters continued to be printed in the Hull Daily Mail even though the recruits were now pouring in to fill the ranks of the East Yorkshire Regiment. The Vicar of Holy Trinity, Mr. George Buchanan, urged Hull's young men to enlist as the war might last longer than expected. [21] In one recruiting notice it was stated that all speakers at public meetings should make it perfectly clear that Germany was striking through France and that England was her objective. [22]

On 6th September the Hull City Hall was opened as a recruiting centre, with Mr. Douglas Boyd as recruiting officer. Mr. Boyd was granted a Commission as Lieutenant for this purpose. [23] The exterior of the City Hall was decked with posters, flags and bunting and the balcony was used for military bands and patriotic speeches. A meeting was held in the Hall on the night of September 8th and was addressed by Lord Curzon and attended by many other Hull dignitaries.

By September 8th the Commercial Battalion was up to strength, but as the recruits still came in it was decided to form a Trades Battalion. This would comprise tradesmen only, welders, joiners, etc. Robert Harris Weasenham joined this unit on the 8th; he was a welder living in East Hull and had no doubts as to the reason he joined up:

> "We joined to save little Belgium and France." [24]

Ernest Land also joined for patriotic reasons; when asked many years later about his reason for enlisting he said, "I wanted to go to be a soldier for my country do you see". Ernest was working at Low Farm, Welton, near the railway line, when a train full of soldiers went by and he said to himself, "It looks like a good job does that, I'm having a go." He left his work and his horse and without telling anyone went straight to Hull City Hall and joined up. He was a seasoned hand with horses even though he was only a farm labourer and was later put in the transport section. Medicals were given on the spot and Edward went upstairs and stripped off:

"We was in the City Hall right up at top in our birthday suits, the lasses (opposite) were looking through the window at us. Tommy Baker said 'Look at them cheeky sods watching us' and waved at them." [25]

When Ernest had enlisted into the 2nd Hull Pals he went back and told his employer, who was not pleased to lose him. His only comment was, "You could have put yer 'oss away couldn't yer." [25] The Trades Battalion was formed within three days recruiting at the City Hall. Recruits still came forward and because of the success of the Commercial and Trades Battalions a third athletes unit was to be raised. Advertisements appeared in the <u>Hull Daily Mail</u> asking for a thousand athletes and other followers of sport:

"If you mean to play the game join at once." [26]

On Saturday, 12th September, a meeting was held at the Artillery Barracks, Park Street, to appeal directly to sportsmen and sports enthusiasts to fill the ranks of the new Battalion. This gathering was addressed by F. S. Jackson, a Yorkshire cricketer who had served in South Africa: "If there is anyone in this country who feels he must kick something, all I can say is let him go to the front, he will have plenty of opportunities of kicking something there." [26]

Advertisements appeared in the <u>Hull Daily Mail</u> at regular intervals appealing for ex-N.C.O.'s for the new Battalions. Age was no obstacle and even men over 45 would be considered. They would not be expected to serve overseas and could serve in their old regiments. The expertise of these ex-servicemen was needed to train the newly assembled 'Pals Battalions' as all soldiers of experience had been sent to the front to swell the ranks of a now badly-depleted B.E.F.

On 17th September the following recruiting figures appeared in the <u>Hull Daily Mail</u>:

Wenlock Barracks	- 1,600
Pryme Street Recruiting Office	- 800
Londsborough Barracks	- 400 (4th East Yorkshire)
Commercials	- 1,020
Tradesmen	- 1,020
Athletes	- 400
Hull Heavy Battery	120
East Hull Depot	- 300

The Commercial Battalion parades. Wenlock Barracks, September 1914

Men of the Commercials in relaxed mood, September 1914

To maintain the momentum of the recruiting drive, a route march for men already enlisted in Hull's new Battalions was organized on 3rd October. The march started from Cannon Street at 3.50 p.m. and proceeded through all the main thoroughfares of the city. The photograph in the <u>Hull Daily Mail</u> of that day shows the men marching down Wellington Lane in civilian dress,

31ST DIVISION (NEW ARMY)

Kitchener volunteers made up the 31st Division
Towns and cities in the North of England raised
numerous Battalions, known as 'Pals Battalions'

92 Brigade

10th Battalion, East Yorkshire (Hull Commercials, 1st Hull Pals)
11th Battalion, East Yorkshire (Tradesman's, 2nd Hull Pals)
12th Battalion, East Yorkshire (Sportsman's, 3rd Hull Pals)
13th Battalion, East Yorkshire (4th Hull Pals)

93 Brigade

15th Battalion, West Yorkshire (Leeds)
16th Battalion, West Yorkshire (Bradford)
18th Battalion, West Yorkshire (Bradford)
18th Battalion, Durham Light Infantry

94 Brigade

11th Battalion, East Lancashire (Accrington)
12th Battalion, Yorkshire and Lancashire (Sheffield)
13th Battalion, Yorkshire and Lancashire (Barnsley)
14th Battalion, Yorkshire and Lancashire (Barnsley)

Divisional Pioneer Battalion

12th Battalion, King's Own Yorkshire Light Infantry

the only distinguishing mark being their arm bands that denoted their particular Battalion. Not one man is bare headed: all are wearing boaters, flat caps or bowlers. Mufflers and ties are also worn by all. The crowds cheered the volunteers enthusiatically and turned out in great numbers all over the city to see Kitchener's men march by.

The route march had the desired effect and the Sportsmen's Battalion was soon up to strength and drilling in Pearson Park. The recruiting was going so well that Lord Nunburnholme received permission from Lord Kitchener to raise a fourth Hull Service Battalion and on 12th November an advertisement appeared in the <u>Hull Daily Mail</u> asking for volunteers to fill the ranks. Albert Barker joined the fourth Service Battalion for a break from routine and for some excitement. "Didn't they all?" he said when questioned about this. His employers thought it marvellous he should go to defend his country. His parents were fervent royalists and were not perturbed when he enlisted:

"The vast majority of people were very patriotic in those days." [27]

When Albert arrived at the Hull City Hall he found many men already there enlisting in the various units. Many lied about their age: birth certificates were not asked for and many underaged lads were later reclaimed by their mothers:

"They took anybody." [27]

Albert Barker in 1914. Albert served in the 13th East Yorks, 1914-1918. He was wounded and taken prisoner on the Somme 13th November, 1916. He still lives in Cottingham, near Hull, and has been a major source of information

Recruiting sergeants often purposely encouraged boys who were under-aged or men who were overaged to enlist. Barker speaks of boys well under the age limit serving with him in France and one man who was 52. The army's physical requirements were also waived at times in order to fill the ranks.

A friend of Barker's who was an inch too short was told by the recruiting sergeant to take a run round the pier and come back as he may have grown by them. He returned later and was allowed to join up.

Because any able-bodied man was allowed to join the 4th Service Battalion it was not thought to be as exclusive as the other three. Albert Barker felt there was much snobbery between the Battalions, especially from the Commercials. Ernest Land of the 2nd Hull Pals also felt the Commercial Battalion considered themselves superior to the others:

"They was all the nobs Battalion, the Commercials used to snob you a bit, they was all clerks and teachers." [28]

The 4th Hull Pals pose for the camera, 1914

By December 9th, Hull could boast four full strength Service Battalions, without weapons, without uniforms and without barracks. But they all had one thing in common: they were keen and eager to play their part in the struggle that lay ahead. The hardships of the future were still an unknown quantity as the city was swept along on a wave of enthusiasm. None of the young men who rushed to the recruiting offices in September had any idea of the kind of conflict they were in for. Neither is there any reason to suppose, had they known, that they would have held back. Men enlisted for many reasons, but in September, 1914, the case for intervention was clear to most of the Hull recruits, that being the defence of Western Europe and of the British way of life that was being threatened by one of the greatest military powers on earth.

Friends and workmates enlisted in batches so that they might serve together:

> "Thirty young men at Kirkella finished work at breakfast-time and marched in one body to Hull and enlisted in the army." [29]

Robert Harris Weasenham, 11th East Yorks 1914-1917. Wounded in the attack on Oppy Wood, 3 May 1917. Died in Hull, 1968. Olive Bertha Weasenham. Died in Hull, February 1990. Grandparents of the author

Many of the new recruits lived in the same street or terrace. This was to make the losses of the next four years even more keenly felt by the Hull community. Each street in Hull was to have its own roll of honour to commemorate the young men who answered the call and never returned. One such roll still exists in Sharp Street, Newland Avenue; now glazed over to protect it from graffiti, it goes unseen by the majority of people who pass it by. The new units had no background or tradition at all, only that of the East Yorkshire Regiment which took them over. The titles such as "The Hull Commercials" that the units gave themselves were never forgotten. The men of the Hull Battalions were proud to be called Kitchener's men and there was great prestige in being one of the chosen.

In January, 1915, Olive Bertha Dawson was walking to town from Nornabell Street with her friend Fanny Mathews, to make up a foursome with Maurice Lumb and Robert Harris Weasenham. When the girls, then 16 years old, reached their destination Robert was in uniform as he had joined the 'Tradesmen's Battalion'. Robert and Olive saw each other regularly and married in December that same year. Olive says of that time:

"He was so smart and handsome in his uniform, I was quite taken with him. I was so proud to walk down the street with him, all heads turned. But I dare not take him home as he had a German sounding name and my father was very strict." [30]

The young soldiers of Hull in 1914 could afford to relax for the time being and enjoy the admiration of the rest of the population, but soon it would be time to transform these would-be soldiers into a Division of fighting men capable of inflicting punishment upon a yet unseen enemy. The Hull Service Battalions were raring to go despite any apprehensions individuals might have held. They had joined on a wave of enthusiasm and patriotism, some for a change and adventure, others because their mates had enlisted; but all had answered the call to do a practical job even though no-one had any idea of the rigours that lay before them.

NOTES

1. The Hull Times. March 14th, 1914.
2. The 1st East Yorkshire were named the Snappers because of an incident from the American War of Independence at the Battle of Brandywine, 1777. During the action ball ammunition ran short, and it is said the officer in command of the 15th Foot, finding out why the advance had paused, roared out "Then snap and be damned to you!".
3. Col. Benson. Killed — Battle of the Aisne, September, 1914. (D.O.W.)
4. The Hull Times. March 14th, 1914. p.8.
5. Thorpe, G. Diary. July 1914. Estate Agent (Architect and Surveyor), National Caledonian Insurance Co., 1 St. Margarets Chambers, Lowgate, Hull. Lived at 2 Rose Villas, Alexandra Road, Hull. Born 1847, died 1939).
6. Denis, G. K.R.R.C. 1914-1918. Taped interview (Author's collection).
7. Thorpe, G. Diary. September, 1914.
8. Hull Daily Mail. August 5th, 1914.
9. Ibid. August 17th, 1914.
10. Ibid. August 25th, 1914.
11. Knightley, D. The First Casualty. (Quartet Books, 1978). p.70.
12. Hull Daily Mail. August 26th, 1914.
13. Ibid. August 27th, 1914.
14. Thorpe, G. Diaries. 28th August, 1914.
15. Hebb, C. Letters (Author's collection). Buried in Hedon Road Cemetery.
16. Hull Daily Mail. 31st August, 1914.
17. Pearson, R. Pte. 10/1180. Hull Commercials, 1915-1918. Diary. (Author's collection).
18. Hull Daily Mail. September, 1914.
19. Ibid. 1st September, 1914.
20. Ibid. 5th September, 1914.
21. Ibid. 10th September, 1914.
22. Ibid. 8th September, 1914.
23. Sheppard, T. Kingston Upon Hull, Before, During and After The Great War. (A. Brown & Sons, 1919). p.95.
24. Weasenham, R. H. Pte. 11/682, 11th East Yorkshires. 1914 — 1917. Conversation with author, 1960's.
25. Land, E. Pte. 11/648. 11th East Yorkshires. Taped interview, 1989. (Author's collection).
26. Hull Daily Mail. September 14th, 1914.
27. Barker, Albert. Taped interview, 1988 (Author's collection).
28. Land, E. 11/648. Pte. 11th East Yorkshires. Taped interview, 1989. (Author's collection).
29. Thorpe, G. Diary. August 29th, 1914.
30. Weasenham, Olive Bertha. Born Hodgeson Street, Hull, 9th November, 1899 (Formerly Dawson). Married R. H. Weasenham, 1st December, 1915. Died February, 1990, in the Kingston General Hospital, Hull, just after this study was completed. (Grandparents of Author).

CHAPTER FOUR

Training

ALL THE YOUNG MEN who joined Hull's Service Battalions were paid one shilling a day from the moment they signed, plus two shillings a day billeting allowance as they were staying in their own homes for the time being. The great numbers of new men enlisting could not be catered for at army depots as they did not have the facilities to house and feed so many.

Uniforms were not available and any rifles that could be acquired were used for teaching recruits how to aim properly and how to keep a weapon in working order. Drilling in the early days took place in civilian dress and the men were taught the basic drill movements. Any open space that was available was used by the new units as they began the long job of turning a bunch of civilians into a disciplined force. The fairground in Walton Street, West Park and the Grammar School playing fields resounded to the sound of marching feet and shouting men.

Retired officers of the Regular or Territoral forces and pensioned N.C.O.'s of the Regular Army, who had responded to Kitchener's appeal, trained the new Service Battalions. The ranks of each unit were combed to find men with any previous military or other training that might make them suitable to become N.C.O.'s. These men were put in charge of smaller units within each Battalion.

At the end of November khaki uniforms were issued to the Hull men and in December they were given the official titles of 10th, 11th, 12th and 13th Battalions of the East Yorkshire Regiment. Together they formed the 92nd Brigade (Infantry), one of three Brigades that made up the 31st Division. This was the largest body of Hull men ever to fight together and, because of its local character, was to make the losses of the war even more keenly felt by the Hull community.

The 10th Battalion was called upon in 1914 to perform the task of coastal duty, as the fear of invasion along the East Coast was very real to the inhabitants of Yorkshire early in the war. By the summer of 1915 all four Hull Battalions had left the City and had marched to their individual barracks in the Ripon — York — Harrogate area.

Men of the Commercials in billets. Hornsea, 1915

Men of the Commercials on coastal duty at Atwick, near Hornsea

Once the troops were established in their new camps the real work of becoming soldiers began in earnest, though much of the routine work seemed to have little to do with ejecting the Germans from Belgium as men took their turn at peeling potatoes, polishing floors and cleaning out latrines plus all the other menial tasks necessary to keep an army in working order.

The recruits were for the most part city-bred and one of the first tasks of the authorities was to bring them up to a state of physical fitness that would enable them to transport themselves, by means of their own two feet, over great distances. The route march was used with great frequency as a tool to toughen the troops and build up their stamina and esprit-de-corps. Photographs taken at the time show the Hull units marching in hot weather, hats pushed to the backs of their heads and rifles resting on their shoulders in a careless fashion, all smiling at the photographer.

As well as marching, much of the work undertaken by the army was hard and physical. All ammunition and provisions had to be moved manually to forward positions and all defensive works, or trenches, had to be dug. The siting and construction of trench works capable of withstanding an artillery barrage was to be of great importance in the coming months. The early shortages of arms and equipment gave the men plenty of time for physical training to bring them up to a standard of fitness that would allow them to perform these arduous tasks.

As entire units were issued with rifles, recruits were instructed in the care and use of the infantryman's best friend, as it was known. Men were taught to think of their rifle as being part of them and it was a crime to neglect their weapon. At first the bulk of a rifle was hard to manage, but men soon got used to it and could, at the word of command, aim kneeling, standing and lying, reload and squeeze the trigger without jerking. When each individual had mastered his weapon training he would then train as part of a section so that the fire of the whole group could be concentrated against the enemy once detected. When live ammunition became available long sessions were spent on the firing ranges as it was of great importance that the men of Kitchener's Army came up to the standards of the regular troops, that is fifteen aimed rounds a minute. As we have seen, when faced with such deadly fire at Mons, the German army had assumed they were being halted by machine-gun fire.

Drill is of prime importance to the army and serves a variety of purposes. Its main aim, however, is to merge the individuals within the ranks into one large unit, so that they will move as one, with one mind and with one purpose. When first being instructed in arms the individual will act on command as well as he is able, but beyond this recruits must train in units involving increasing numbers of men. In order to encourage the recruit to see himself as one element of a larger whole, he is at first trained in a squad of about 20 men, then a platoon of about 50 men, then in companies consisting of

The 13th East Yorks on a route-march in the Ripon — Harrogate area, looking smart with rifles at the slope

Later that day the 13th East Yorks are looking hot and tired

four platoons and finally in battalions of 1,000 men. Soliders reaching such a high state of training would in battle behave as a unit and go against their natural instincts when facing danger, which for most would be to run away. Drill was the embodiment of military discipline; it taught prompt and methodical obedience, confidence in the other parts of the unit and pride in that unit. In this way men who were far from the field of battle were conditioned to behave in a disciplined manner and act as a cohesive whole, capable of rapid movement, and to behave in such a way even when under fire.

Battle training concepts at the start of World War One were based on obsolete tactics that were out of date at the time of the Boer War and before. The main role of the infantry was to close with the enemy as soon as possible. Lines of troops would advance in leap-frog style. One line would advance, stop, give covering fire while the second line passed through them, halted, and in turn covered the next line until the enemy was 200 to 250 yards away. Then would come the massed bayonet attack. In the Infantry Training Manual of 1914 it says of such an assault:

> "During the delivery of the assault the men will cheer, bugles be sounded and pipes played."

This conjures up visions of massed scarlet-clad ranks advancing through the smoke and shot at Waterloo accompanied by banners and bands, and such was the training the Hull men received. They were taught to close with the enemy as soon as possible [1] in order to use the bayonet. No other weapon in the soldier's arsenal demanded the subduing of individual fear and absolute obedience to orders to such an extent. The French in August, 1914, had already suffered massive casualties, running into thousands, by launching massed bayonet attacks against German positions, and the Germans likewise at Mons and Le-Cateau against British lines, but still the same old tactics were being taught to the new armies, tactics that would have been admirable against Napoleon's Imperial Guard, but suicidal in a war already being dominated by high explosive and machine guns. The new Battalions were being poorly prepared for twentieth century warfare. Throughout the war only 0.03 per cent of wounds were inflicted with the bayonet. Looking back many years later Reginald Pearson wrote in his diary:

> "All our training had been with a view to open warfare, extended order, artillery formation and advanced guards as employed in the South African war." [2]

The soldier was the end-product of all this, identical with every other recruit by his uniform and actions. Each day was planned out for him and most of them were the same as the days before. The independently-minded individual had been replaced by a number and a rank that would act with uniformity wherever he was ordered to go. Any individual who would not conform found a host of punitive measures that could be used against him. For minor offences

The 13th East Yorks 'spud-bashing'

The Hull Commercials' Band. Ripon, 1915

men would be put on a charge and then brought to Company Orders; unshined boots or dirty accoutrements would get a man confined to barracks for varying lengths of time, depending on how serious the offence was considered to be. This kind of measure was irritating to men, especially when taken to extremes by an overzealous or downright sadistic N.C.O. or officer. Pte. 11/682 Weasenham of the 11th Battalion described his section coming out of the front line in 1916 and being lined up, still covered in filth, to have their rifles inspected. Most of the men found themselves on a charge and Pte. Weasenham never forgave the officer who carried out this petty action.

The more serious cases would be brought before the Commanding Officer who had the power to stop pay, strip a man of his rank or sentence a man to field punishment number two. The latter would mean a note in the paybook, the forfeiture of pay, sleeping under guard and as many fatigues and drills as possible each day for 28 days. On top of this, the offender would not be allowed to smoke and would be on a diet of water and biscuit.

Field punishment number one was by far the worst and was designed to humiliate a man in full view of his comrades: he would be lashed to a waggon wheel and spreadeagled for two hours each day. Pte. Surfleet of the 13th Battalion describes in his diary deep feelings of indignation that ran to near mutiny in his unit when they came across a soldier lashed to a wheel with his arms and legs wide apart and head falling forward. This was during the Somme campaign and Surfleet cursed the individuals who devised and inflicted such a penalty; he wrote:

> "I dont think I have ever seen anything which so disgusted me in my life." [3]

Other men of the 13th possessed a more fatalistic attitude towards the more unpleasant side of army life. Pte. Albert Barker from Cottingham had been in service for some years before joining up and argued that all the volunteers knew they would be subject to army regulations when they joined and had to accept their punishment if they broke the rules:

> "I never grumbled because I volunteered, Can't do owt' about it." [4]

In the coming months the soldiers of Kitchener's Army would come to know far worse when men broke under the strain and were executed for cowardice in the face of the enemy. For these long-forgotten men death would not come on the field of battle, but as the macabre climax of an ancient ritual, all in the name of discipline. Throwing away one's arms and running from the enemy was the most serious of crimes in war and for this men would face a Military Court-Martial. In the whole of the First World War 304,262 men were court-martialled and 346 were known to have suffered the death penalty. As we shall see later, men sentenced to death were shot in an out-of-the-way place with men from their own unit made to watch. Twelve men would be chosen and given a mixture of live and blank ammunition to ease

Hull Pals men queue for a haircut, 1915

*Trench digging was back-breaking work and a frequent event for the
Hull Pals in 1915*

their consciences; an officer with a pistol would stand by to finish off the job if needed. Each of these deaths would be reported to the man's family as killed in action. The Hull Pals never had to carry out this dreadful task though they knew of such things.

In October and early November, 1915, the Hull Units were moved to Salisbury Plain for Divisional training and here they received their first experience of trench life. Taking over trenches at night and holding the line was practised and many years later Pte. Pearson remembered how different these trenches were from the ones they found in France. [5] The men were instructed in how to make home-made bombs from jam and condensed milk tins. Bombing was to be an important skill that was often employed by trench soldiers, though in these early days the bombs were as lethal to their makers as to the enemy:

"It's a wonder we didn't all kill ourselves." [6]

In November, 1915, the new Small Model Lee-Enfield rifle was issued to the troops and the men began to get used to their new weapon as the time for their departure from England drew ever nearer. When asked 70 years later if he felt as though his training had prepared him for what he found in France, Gerald Denis answered, "It prepared us for nothing." [7]

9 Platoon, 'C' Company, 11th East Yorks, 1915. Third from the left in the third row from the back is Cpl Peter McNally, later R.S.M., 1/4th East Yorks

The business of training Hull's Service Battalions took from December, 1914, to December, 1915. During this period of intensive training much sorting out took place and men who were capable of commanding respect and obedience rose to the rank of N.C.O. and even junior officers. Men of above-average intelligence became signallers and scouts. Those that were handy with their hands were picked as machine-gunners, lewis-gunners or joined the transport section. By the time the winter of 1915 came around the novelty had worn off and fighting mock battles with blank shells and blank rifle ammunition had become routine. All the drills and formations had been learned by heart, the four Battalions could dig, act on orders without prompting, release 15 rounds a minute rapid fire, live off the land and take their sleep when the opportunity presented itself.

They had participated in mock actions involving the whole 31st Division without disaster; these manoeuvres involved great numbers of infantrymen plus the headquarters staff, cavalry, artillery, ammunition columns, transport train signallers and field ambulances. All was simulated that could be without actually doing battle, but would this be much different from the real thing? The men of the 31st Division did not know, but as they moved from Salisbury Plain to an unknown destination the Hull men were somewhat apprehensive but eager to play their part in the great struggle.

NOTES

1. Infantry Training Manual. August, 1914. p.134.
2. Pearson, R. Pte. 10/1180. Hull Commercials. 1915-1918. Diary. (Author's collection).
3. Wilson, T. Myriad Faces of War. (Polity, 1986). p.358.
4. Pte. Albert Barker. Taped interview, 1988. (Author's collection).
5. Pearson, R. Diary.
6. Ibid.
7. Denis, G. K.R.R.C. 1915-1918. Taped interview, 1989. (Author's collection).

Pals Battalions leave England for the East, 1915

CHAPTER FIVE

Egyptian Interlude
December 1915 — March 1916

E ARLY IN DECEMBER, 1915 the Hull Battalions, wearing pith helmets, boarded their transports in Devonport naval base. As the ships left the harbour other ships at anchor lowered their flags in salute. The weather was cold and frosty but the men made the most of their second-class berths as they left the shores of England, most of them for the first time like 11/682 Pte. Weasenham, who had never been out of Yorkshire. All letters home were now subject to strict censorship for obvious reasons.

Ships travelled in complete darkness except for the Red Cross ships which were brilliantly lit at night; destroyers glided alongside the troop-ships to protect them from attack. The worst part of the voyage was the seasickness that afflicted these landlubbers and laid most of them low for a time:

"For two whole days I was seasick, swinging in a hammock as were most of the others." [1]

wrote Pte. Carter of the Commercials. On the deck below him were the animals, hundreds of mules and horses, that gave off a most pungent smell. They suffered far worse than the men: several of them died and had to be thrown overboard. Fatigues, guards and drills occupied the men on the outward voyage and there were many submarine alerts but little else to do. Late in December the Hull units found themselves in a hot sunny climate as they docked in Alexandria Harbour.

The men celebrated Christmas Day in boiling hot weather and began to get acclimatised to their new environment. Their opinon of the native population was not high:

"The scum of about six nations seems to be collected there, so you really need an assorted mouthful of languages to get along. In default of this a few good oaths said with spirit and a hefty stick laid lustily about the varlets' backs will work wonders." [2]

All supplies had to be guarded with great care as the natives of the local towns, who were very poor and lived by their wits, would have them in an instant:

Officers and men of the Hull Pals pose for the camera

Pith helmets help to protect men from the hot sun. Note that some are still wearing cloth caps.

"Thieves, I've never met the like. If you turn your back to sign the invoice, the chances are one of your packages has gone." [2]

The troops often paid visits to the towns in the area even though at times they were not supposed to. The men were not allowed out on their own as it was too dangerous: Pte. Weasenham remembers that bayonets were always carried to defend themselves against the locals. The brothels were in the poorer areas of Alexandria and although out of bounds were frequently visited by the troops.

Lack of money was a problem and Albert Barker recalls how they supplemented their meagre pay:

"When the natives were in the camp we would sell them our surplus equipment, when they tried to leave our mates in the guard room would take them off them, this was the only way we got any extra money." [3]

The tommies, not having a high opinion of the locals, viewed them as fair game and swindled money off them regularly in this way.

The Hull units had been brought to the East to guard the Suez Canal from Turkish attack and each one of the four Battalions, along with the rest of the 31st Division, took up their positions and waited. Working parties were constantly hard at it as cleanliness and sanitation were of paramount importance in such a hot climate, but there were many new sights to see and lots of new wildlife upon the nearby waters. At night the men would watch the great ships passing along the canal:

"Our main amusement is watching ships sailing through the canal, it's a fine sight at night when each ship carries a searchlight in her bows that lights up the whole canal like day. You can see them coming for miles." [4]

When Ernest Land of the 11th East Yorkshires had time off he loved to spend it in the canal. Wearing only his helmet, he would stand up to his neck in water and enjoy a cigarette while watching Dutch ships sail by. [5]

During the day, organizing the camel drivers was a major task for the officers when any movement of troops took place, which was quite often. Pte. Weasenham spoke of men being bitten by these strange and unruly creatures. Capt. Williams wrote home:

"The camel drivers are a great nuisance. We have 80 camels here in our camp and 300 more close by — now and then they go wild — one killed his driver yesterday." [4]

Food consisted of bully beef and army biscuits, sometimes accompanied by a portion of jam or butter, but some of the more inventive tommies supplemented their diets with fish from the canal and some of the officers with game from the surrounding area. From noon until about three in the afternoon little was done because of the heat but men could often be seen in a state of undress burning out the sand-lice from their clothes:

11th East Yorks machine-gun section

Camels and their driver

"Sand-lice became part and parcel of our life and a constant source of irritation." [6]

The time spent in Egypt was uneventful, like the voyage there and the voyage home, as the expected Turkish attack never came, but events in Europe were on the move and the soldiers of the 31st Division were now needed for the big push being planned by the Allies. Pte. Carter of the Commercials looked back upon his Egyptian interlude many years later and recalled:

"It was a lovely war and came to an end too soon." [7]

In Early March, 1916, the Hull Battalions arrived at Marseilles in cold, bleak weather to begin their real war service, though none of them had an inkling of what was in store for them in the summer of 1916.

NOTES

1. Carter, Pte. Hull Commercials, 1915. Diary. (Author's collection).
2. Williams, E. C. Capt. Letters from Egypt, 1916. (Author's collection).
3. Barker, A. 13th East Yorkshires. 1914-1918. Taped interview, 1988. (Author's collection).
4. Williams, E. C. Letters.
5. Land, E. Pte. 11/648, 11th East Yorkshires, 1914-1918. Taped interview, 1989. (Author's collection).
6. Pearson, R. Pte. 10/1180, Hull Commercials, 1915-1918. Diary. (Author's collection).
7. Carter, Diary.

CHAPTER SIX

The Promise of Tragedy, 1916

I N EARLY MARCH the troopships carrying the Hull Pals slipped into Marseilles harbour. The weather could not have been more of a contrast from Egypt with the icy winter winds blowing rain and snow across the terrain of Southern France. Once off their transports the troops had to wait on the exposed quayside; many years later Pte. Pearson of the Commercials recalled that long wait:

> "We all felt shrivelled up and would have felt more so had we known what awaited us at the end of that frightful journey." [1]

At last the train arrived to transport them to the battle zone. It was a very basic affair with wooden seats, and men were packed eight to a compartment with kit and rifles. This was to be their home for over 48 hours as the train crawled along, sometimes at walking pace, passing such places as Lyons, Dijon and Versailles, but the men were living in such poor conditions and had to put up with such intense cold that little interested them:

> "It all seemed such a nightmare after England and Egypt." [2]

The journey was long and tedious; men would take it in turns to run or walk at the side of the train to get warm and, when the train stopped, would rush to the engine to get boiling water for tea and other hot drinks. Only towards the end of the second day was any food provided, and this was very meagre. The troops detrained at Port Remy in a snow storm and marched off to an unknown destination in the pitch-black night.

The troops marched six miles and arrived at Longpre suffering from hunger, lack of sleep and bitter cold, but after the confusion of the first night in their new home the men became used to the fresh surroundings of the Somme Valley.

Now came the work of hardening up these inexperienced Battalions who as yet had seen no fighting and who had become soft after their easy time in the East. Trench warfare had now taken over the whole front and while many of the Kitchener units were now hardened trench-soldiers, the men of the 31st Division had to be eased into a way of fighting that was completely alien to them. Intensive training began once again as the Hull boys practised bayonet fighting, musketry, bombing and gas drill with the new-type helmets then in use. Once more the route march became the prime tool in bringing the men up the required standard of fitness. After the soft sands of Egypt the cobbled roads of France played havoc with the soldiers' feet:

> "Men were falling out right and left with blistered and sore feet. Evidently Egypt has not done us much good, for every man was exhausted when we reached Longpre again." [3]

In this period selected officers and N.C.O.'s visited the front line, then after nearly three days' march the Hull Battalions followed them. As the men approached the front the landscape became more desolate, whole villages were in ruins and the hardware of war was everywhere — ammunition dumps, masses of artillery and limbers, barbed wire, trenches and dressing stations. As the Hull Commercials approached the front the boom of the German heavy guns could be heard a long way off and Pte. Graystone thought it "not a very pleasant sound." [4]

The night before taking over the front line was spent at Engelbelmer. Flares lit up the surrounding countryside and the roar of the guns and chatter of machine guns did not disturb the men's sleep as they were exhausted after their long march. But not all the men were lucky enough to sleep, as some were called upon for gas guard. At the door of each billet was hanging a used shell case which the guard would strike with his bayonet is he saw gas coming towards him. Pte. Pearson stepped out on duty never having seen gas in his life, let alone a gas attack:

> "How do I recognise whether it is gas or just smoke?" [5]

As he stood there he watched with interest the blazing flares and flashes from the guns; machine guns occasionally joined in and a lone bullet whistled past him. It was all rather eerie and Pearson was glad when his relief came so he could sleep at last.

On March 27th, the 10th and 11th Battalions took over a section of the line in front of Beaumont Hamel. The trench systems were to be where men would see their most dangerous service. The front line consisted of three parallel lines: the fire trench, the travel trench at 20 yards and finally the support line. All the lines were constructed in zig-zag shape with bays at intervals so as to minimize bomb blasts and to prevent enemy troops enfilading the trench should a raiding party enter it. The depth of trenches was about four feet with a built-up wall of sandbags as a parapet to allow men to stand up. Ideally a trench would have a floor of duckboards, under which drains and sumps would be dug to get rid of water. Old soldiers would laugh at this description as most British trenches on the western front, in the winter months, would be knee deep and deeper in rain water with no hope of any relief from this particular form of misery:

> "The mud however did not stop us from doing a heavy day's bombing in the dilapidated trenches nearby. We were covered with mud from head

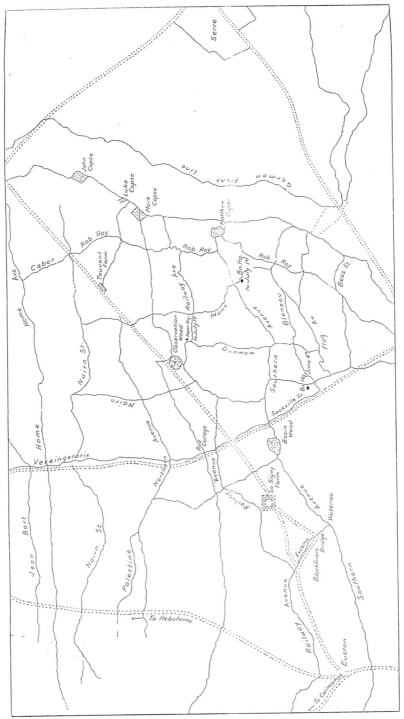

10th Battalion Front to 1st July, 1916

to foot when we finished." [6]

Facing the enemy was a step, the fire step: from here the men could fire on any advancing enemy troops. Of the 20,000 men in a division only 2,000 would be in the front line at any one time. Men rarely fought for long periods of time and the 11th Battalion's front-line stint lasted only 3 days, but the tension of the front-line soldier, who could expect death to descend at any moment, made it seem a lot longer. In future months the Hull units would be expected to withstand this pressure for far longer tours of duty. Some sections of the line would be quiet sectors where men went about their repairs and daily routines, others would be much more active with constant shelling, sniping and raiding.

The Hull units were being inducted into the trenches as a preliminary to the July offensive. The troops they would have to face would be battle-hardened infantry who had never suffered a major defeat. The Pals of the 31st Division were green by comparison and had never experienced an assault on an entrenched position, whereas the men they faced had perfected their trade in the hard school of battle. The promise of tragedy hung in the air.

When in the line the men could not wear great-coats; packs would be left behind and haversacks stuffed with necessities. If the weather was icy sheep-skins, cardigans and fingerless gloves would be crammed in with all the other material needed for trench warfare.

A very rare photograph of three men of the 11th East Yorks in a dug-out at the front. The man on the right wearing a sheepskin is Lt. Jack Harrison v.c., killed at the Battle of Oppy Wood, 3rd May, 1917.

The timetable in the front line was fixed: half an hour before dawn would come the stand-to, when all men would stand to arms on the fire step. This was supposed to be the time when the enemy was at his most dangerous. At dawn the men stood down and sentries were posted. In the trench, fields of fire would be checked, along with stores and the state of the trench itself. After this would come breakfast, the cleaning of rifles and possibly the killing of lice in the seams of tunics.

There was always work to do, filling sandbags, digging, draining water, strengthening the wire, etc. At dusk the men stood to once more before the onset of darkness when ration parties supplied much-needed labour to help with fatigues. The fall of darkness brought with it great activity and was interspersed with gun flashes, the gleam of star shells that lit up the whole area and the scream of shells or the chatter of machine-gun fire. German night raids were a constant fear to troops already edgy; men on sentry duty would see phantom shapes in the flashes and glares cast across a torn-up landscape. Fear gripped the men as they did their best to cope with the long hours on duty. One night in 1916 Pte. Weasenham and a pal were on sentry duty on a dark and gloomy night and felt quite isolated in their section of trench. Two men came out of no-man's-land dressed in British khaki with the insignia of the Duke of Wellington's Regiment. They were duly challenged and having answered in perfect English they were allowed to enter the trench and were questioned. Both sentries were aware there had been no activity in the area and the Duke of Wellingtons were not in this sector, but in the darkness fear took over and they were both pleased to allow the strangers to pass. The next day no mention from the rear was made of the incident and the two sentries never told anyone about it. [7]

An even more severe test for the men was night patrolling, with the aim of curbing enemy patrol activity and seeing if anything was afoot in the German lines. All who went on such patrols were volunteers.

The men who took part had to be ruthless and would be well known to each other. Faces would be blacked and bayonets dulled, bowie knives, home-made clubs and grenades would be carried, though the latter were for emergencies only as any noise in no-man's-land meant star shells and the inevitable spray of machine-gun bullets cutting across the landscape just above ground level. Albert Barker of the 13th Battalion (4th Hull Pals) looked back on this particular activity in 1988 with the comment:

"Night patrols, worse than battle." [8]

Day or night the enemy was rarely seen and each side would piece together a picture of its opponents by the sounds heard as men went about their daily routines. Working party routes, patrol habits and machine-gun positions were all known. Pte. Weasenham remembers hearing Germans walking on duckboards, talking and laughing with each other. Shells would come over

A barrage at night was a spectacular sight, although few would stay around to enjoy the fireworks

at a certain time during the day to show the opposing side that their range had been found and any strafing would mean retaliation:

> "If we send a bomb into their trenches they send half a dozen into ours, if we wish to remain quiet the enemy will do the same." [9]

All these details would enable opposing sides to construct a mental picture of the enemy and though he was seldom seen the overall feeling was one of constant danger. In training the men had not been prepared for long periods of inactivity, at the same time having to be vigilant while living a subterranean existence, walking with a stoop and having to be aware of the many forms of danger that threatened life at all times and demanded constant care.

Fear and tension kept men alive: anyone relaxing for a moment and showing himself would be picked off by the ever-waiting sniper. These were the real killers during times of inactivity and the marksmanship of these hard professional soldiers was marvelled at by the British troops. They worked behind the front line, though some would be in camouflaged suits in no-man's-land. The one way to dislodge a sniper was to obtain a rough bearing by listening to the report of the rifle and observing the angle of the incoming bullet. By drawing his fire at various points soldiers could work out where he was hidden and flush him out. In the summer of 1916 Pte. Weasenham was in a very quiet sector and he and his pals passed the time away by popping up dummies that were promptly shot by the local sniper but after a while they became bored with this. Hours later a young officer looked into no-man's-land from the same trench and received a bullet through the throat. Pte. Weasenham remembered the gargling noise the man made as he died:

> "We all felt very sorry for him as he was well liked by all the men."

Snipers would wait for hours to get their prey and once seen a man had little chance to escape from these deadly accurate marksmen.

The popular civilian view of the Great War was one of great battles involving thousands of men rushing forward in true Boys' Own style, of artillery duels and raids. Old soldiers looking back after many years recall how rarely these actions interrupted long periods of stagnation and boredom. The enemy most often seen and felt by them was the weather, from which there was no escape or relief. No matter what precautions men might take, the cold penetrated to the bone and made night duties especially dreaded in the winter months. Rain, snow and mud gave them no respite and made life in an open trench unbearable:

> "Raining every day since we have been back in the trenches. Mud worse than ever in this part. We stand in the open trench all night. Everyone is so miserable." [10]

Living in such cramped unhygienic conditions for long periods of time meant that vermin were inevitable; big black flies would infest the front in great swarms as the available rotting corpses in no-man's-land provided a perfect breeding ground. They would cover sand bags and trench sides, and at High Wood in November, 1916, Lt. Cecil Slack saw a gruesome sight. From a distance he thought the smashed tree stumps were covered in tar as they were so black; upon closer scrutiny he found they were covered with big black bluebottles in their thousands:

> "It was not tar but a crawling mass of bluebottle flies, millions of them, you would see them crawling in and out of the holes of empty skulls." [11]

Rats would also colonize the front and grew unusually large and brazen as they scuttled about, making a good living on the waste products left by the troops and the rotting meat provided by dead bodies. Ratting was a popular sport for men in quiet sectors; Lt. Slack considered this sport good training for the eye and employed a knobbed stick that he found to be quite effective. Writing home to a friend he declared, "The rats here are as big as tigers" [12] and spoke of one that lived in his dugout and stole various items if left out, dragging them to its home at the foot of Slack's bed:

> "There is one who lives near the foot of my bunk. This one practices the long jump over my legs, and trains for the hundred yards up and down my body." [13]

But the biggest tribulation common to all front line troops was the body louse. In looks these were like tiny white lobsters and had the habit of feeding ten times daily; they would hold on to cloth fibres and drink blood. Lice could breed quickly and left eggs in the seams of uniforms. Men would spend time in quiet sectors burning lice out of the seams of their tunics with a candle or lighter:

> "It was new clothing but was infested with lice. I dealt with these in the usual way, using a lighted cigarette to cremate them. We could never get rid of these body lice." [14]

The combined effects of a poor diet, vermin and the wet and cold produced illness of various kinds. Dysentry, frostbite, nephritis and pneumonia increased. Only if a man was about to collapse was he admitted to hospital, otherwise it would be a tablet and back to normal duties.

All diaries written by the men of the Hull Pals talk of the lack of sleep when in the line. The exposed positions of the infantry in the forward area prevented any long period of sleep and the dozes that were snatched were brief, as the constant noise and cold of the front woke men up after a short time. All modern experiments in sleep deprivation show how lack of sleep produces irrationality of thought and complete changes in character within the individual. Men would become unpredictable and slow. The life below ground and the sameness of routine added to this sense of lack of purpose:

> "I awoke feeling miserable and dissatisfied, for is not today a Bank holiday? No holiday for us though. Every day is like its predecessor and very often worse!" [15]

Officers usually slept in a dug-out but the men were lucky if they had a hole in the trench side to rest in. All this slowly wore them down but if a dug-out was found it was a rare event:

> "Still raining, troops in very bad condition, we are covered from head to foot with mud. As a rest we spend three hours in the cook's dug-out which is a delightful treat." [16]

Food was constantly on the minds of men who were always hungry. When in the line it could be delayed for many reasons: poor administration, shells falling in the rear or on communication trenches and the ever-present mud. The rum ration was always appreciated at the morning stand-down by most men. It was strong stuff and cheered them up after a night of cold or rain or both. This would be consumed before the issuing officer to prevent pooling. Tea and cigarettes were available most times and would give troops something that seemed to alleviate their sufferings and make it all bearable. In the killing zone where high explosive reigned supreme, inessentials were not tolerated and men never took with them anything that was not vital to their trade or their comfort.

At times nature would remind some men of the gentler side of their humanity. In an area devoid of women or children, animals had a particular place in their affections. It is well documented how dogs and cats found in the area would be adopted by troops and how soldiers in transport sections soon became attached to individual horses. Birds too were a constant pleasure to most men. One day in 1916 Pte. Tait had been on a working party that lasted for 15 days far behind the front line. On Tuesday, May 2nd, he returned to his billet and went for a ramble that evening in some nearby woods. The contrast to the battle zone was so great that he marvelled at the trees' green mantle and the peacefulness of the area:

> "The sun is sinking in the west, the lurid sky giving a beautiful effect to the picturesque countryside. The birds are in full song." [17]

Cuckoos and thrushes sang and enhanced this moment of respite in this young man's war:

> "As in the firing line the larks mock the efforts of men whose object is slaughter. When we shelter in this peaceful harbour we think how absurd it is to be at war and how the folly of it all is brought home to us." [18]

For the first time in military history a war was being fought that did not cease hostilities during the winter months. At the front, noise of one sort or another was constant and even way back in base camp men could hear the constant boom of the heavy guns. As troops approached the front the sounds became more audible and men would soon be able to pick out the various types of weapon purely by sound and act accordingly. Each man knew that every explosion could mean personal mutilation or death and it was his reaction to them that would help keep him alive, or at least enhance his chances

Commercials' Lewis-gun section. Doullens, summer 1916

The <u>sucrerie</u>, near Colincamps, ruined by shelling

of survival.

The enemy artillery was composed of two types: the high muzzle-velocity gun with a shallow trajectory and the howitzer that would fire its large shell much more slowly and in a steep arc. Because of the static nature of most of the Great War large concentrations of big guns were possible and the poor infantry often came under bombardments of massive proportions.

Because of the static nature of the Great War, infantrymen often came under fire from massive artillery formations. Here is one German field-piece in action.

Diaries left by the men of the Hull Pals mention 'Jack Johnsons', (named after the black world heavyweight champion, 1908-15, because of the noise and black smoke emissions), 'Whizz Bangs' (so called because they came out of nowhere and give little warning before exploding above the trench), and 'Piss Tins,[19] (these could have all kinds of metal fragments in them to ensure maximum maiming on impact). These all refer to different kinds of shells that harassed the infantrymen in the line; the one most feared by the troops was the Whizz-Bang because it was the swiftest and gave no time to dive for cover.

"The only shell we really dread is their Whizz-bang, which gives us no warning of its approach. It simply whizzes on the parapet and the next second bangs into the trench."[20]

Shrapnel was a most effective anti-personnel weapon and an air burst, if judged correctly, could explode above exposed troops with a white puff of smoke, forming a pyramid of death 200 yards high and a thousand yards wide at its base. Shrapnel helmets gave little protection to men directly under such a burst and the fragments would inflict ghastly wounds upon men caught in the open. Louis Osborne of the 11th Battalion was on a working party one night carrying tea to the front; the tea urn was on his back when shrapnel burst above the communication trench without warning. He felt the hot tea streaming down his neck; the tea urn was now peppered with holes and he considered himself to be very lucky.

The shell least feared was the kind that came over in bunches at set times just to warn that the enemy was alert and ready for action should the need arise. Aerial and balloon observation meant that each side had a detailed picture of the enemy lines and rear areas. Spots such as saps, latrines, mortar positions, etc. were all pinpointed and individual shells would be sent over to these key points; if any major activity was spotted these places would come in for special attention.

All front-line troops had tales to tell of near-misses and lucky escapes from shellfire but they all knew how high explosive and jagged steel could rip apart the bodies of men; if a man was hit directly he would just disintegrate or be found in pieces scattered about:

> "During this bombardment one shell fell into a dugout in which were four men, three were blown into small pieces and the fourth only had his forehead scratched." [21]

Being buried alive was also very much in the minds of men living below ground. Shells exploding outisde a trench could blow in tons of earth on to men crouching to avoid shrapnel and blast. Pte. Weasenham recalls such a time on the Somme in 1916 when one of his mates was buried alive: "We all dug like mad until we got him out, he was alright but had got such a blow on his helmet it had been forced on to his head, his head became swollen and he was sent to the rear to have it removed, we all had a good laugh later." [22]

Over half the wounds by the end of the war were shell wounds; the tearing effect of fragments and splinters would drag foreign matter into the body turning it septic and making men vulnerable to gangrene. Even those who managed to avoid flying fragments of steel were not safe as blast could kill at thirty feet, rupturing kidneys and spleen and leaving no outwardly visible marks.

The real test of a man's self-control came in the barrage, a constant stream of high explosive pummelling trenches and men in an endless outpouring of fire power. Sgt. Arthur Hilton of 1/4th East Yorkshires came under intense shellfire for the first time in May, 1915; his comment in his brief diary reads:

> "Perfect hell upon earth." [23]

A sniper killed him that same month.

Pte. Pearson tried to cope with this ordeal by making a pact with his maker on a dark misty night in 1916 at the Windmill at Gavrelle:

Sgt. Arthur Hilton, 1/4th East Yorks, who was killed by a sniper in May 1915; his body was never found. His son Les was in France in 1940 with the 4th East Yorks and was amazed to find his father's name on the Menin Gate.

> "5-9's falling thick and fast. Up till now I had never thought much about God, but I remember saying 'O God, look after me now and bring me safely through this and I'll be a different and better chap when I get out'." [24]

Men got through this particular hell as best they could. As the 11th Battalion East Yorkshires waited in the reserve trenches on 1st July, 1916, Pte: Weasenham saw men shake with fear during the barrage and felt nothing but pity as others wept, expecting to be sent into no-man's-land after suffering the wrath of the German artillery. That same year in November the Hull Pals were attacking at Serre and after the attack Pte. Pearson describes the result of a heavy bombardment on trenches:

> "My journey took me along a communication trench called Hairsin, which, before the morning attack was a six foot deep trench, well sandbagged and strengthened — its walls were now flattened and the trench was lined with corpses, one on top of another, dead and wounded, some just naked bodies stripped bare by the terrible concussion of the German shells." [25]

He stood there stunned by the sight until forced to move by the attentions of enemy machine-gunners.

Men would have to endure the barrage for hours and even days. Tired and hungry troops would sit amidst this inferno and become oblivious to everything as a feeling of unreality crept over them. With nowhere to hide and no hope of any relief, it became just too much and only the rum ration kept them going, that is when it got to them. Louis Osborne sat with a group of the 11th Battalion in a barrage during the British retreat of 1918 and thought each moment his last as shells rained about his little group, seemingly getting closer each time. The men shook hands, said a prayer and waited for the end:

> "I looked at Stan's face, the horror stricken look, then at Lt. James', also grey and ashen, mine felt the same. — The bombardment roars on. — I become desperate and want to evacuate our position as we were like rats in a trap. About noon we grew oblivious of what was happening, only sat and wondered how long we would last. Home seemed like a dream we had had some far off time ago." [26]

Shelling had a demoralising effect even on brave men; no one escaped its fury and no one was immune from its effects. The men who returned to Hull would have nightmares about it and Pte. Weasenham would flinch at the sound of a loud bang for some time after the war. The Hull Pals had gone abroad with visions of glory and brave deeds; these things were indeed achieved, but many paid the price by being blown to pieces, cruelly maimed or buried alive by high explosive. For these reasons all men feared artillery, and if they escaped injury the mental scars they received took many years to heal. Some never recovered from them.

In 1915 gas made its appearance on the Western Front on the Ypres salient. This was a new development in warfare, yet hideous though it was, it was not able to break the stalemate of the trenches but only added to the list of horrors being suffered by the infantry in the line. 1915 saw great leaps in gas warfare technology. Tear gas came first followed by the more murderous chlorine, phosgene and mustard in 1917. Gas was released from cylinders in the front line up to July, 1916; after that it was despatched in shells or mortar canisters. Men feared this form of death with good reason: if breathed in, it caused death by destryoing the alveoli of the lungs and the smaller bronchial tubes. Men would find themselves unable to absorb oxygen and drown in the water generated in their own lungs.

From the early chlorine was developed phosgene, many times more lethal, and invisible, unlike the green chlorine cloud. When breathed in in sufficient quantity it did not seem to work at once as its effect was delayed. Later would come the drowning spasms as the lungs produced four pints of yellow liquid per hour for 48 hours, the pulse would race and breathing would become shallow. Phosgene casualties were terrible to behold.

Mustard gas came on the scene in 1917. By this time repirators had been provided that could resist gases, but only a small amount was needed to put troops out of action for days. One part of gas to ten million parts of air would make a man feel as though an attack of influenza was on the way: throats would burn and eyes puff up and close. Any flesh that was not protected would become one enormous blister, pulse rate would rocket along with temperature and pneumonia develop. In the worst cases men could be burnt through to the bone, cough up mucous membranes or lose their genitals.

Mustard gas looked like sherry and smelt like onions and once delivered could be trapped in hollows or woods to evaporate slowly; in the winter it would be frozen and when a thaw set in it could have catastrophic effects on unprepared troops.

Men affected by gas guide one another to a casualty clearing station

At the front line opposite Serre in 1916, engineers had dug an underground sap into no-man's-land. Unknown to them the Germans had dug a counter-sap. During the night the Germans broke through into the British tunnel and finding no one in the immediate area pumped in poison gas. The engineers had pulled back along the sap and were sleeping when the gas reached them; only one officer got out to get help. The Hull Commercials were holding the line that night and some of them donned gas helmets and entered the tunnel with bayonets and bombs at the ready:

> "What a sight met our eyes, those poor chaps gasping in what had been their sleep and now frothing at the mouth." [27]

Infantry were not only affected by enemy gas; British counter-gas measures made hard work for the infantry as canisters had to be manhandled to all forward areas. Once on the parapet a favourable wind would be waited for; if the enemy had noticed any activity the men knew it would mean a bombardment. This was a constant fear to those who had to work and sleep with gas day and night.

The Hull Commercials suffered in June, 1916, from their own gas canisters. Gas was released at night, as the Royal Engineers moved down the trench through the Hull men and opened the valves. But instead of the deadly cloud moving towards the enemy positions it drifted back into the British front line. The men holding the line put on their masks quickly but others in dugouts and in shelters got no warning and 'D' Company suffered casualties. The engineers could not be found and there was uproar in the line:

> "I saw a certain sergeant charging up and down the front line, revolver in hand, looking for those adjectival R.E.'s to come and turn the stuff off or else." [28]

Ernest Land of the 11th East Yorkshires was in the transport section and recalled many years later bringing dead men from the front on his horse-drawn waggon; he found it most distressing:

> "Bloody awful, they were blown up like balloons you know." [29]

The weaponry that was used in the Great War was the result of many years of technological development. The ability to transport so many men to one confined area and maintain them was a feat of massive proportions. The many ways in which men were broken and killed on the field of battle were myriad and between March and July, 1916, the Hull Service Battalions were coming to terms with the horrors of life in the trenches. Casualties were constant when in the line and the terminology of their new life-style became a part of their make-up. 'Whizz-Bangs', 'Piss-Tins', 'the wind up' were well known to the generation that served in the Great War and to two generations after them, but now the young know little of these names as they pass into the history books and even the name 'The Great War' is little known among them. But talk to any soldier of 1914-1918 and he will talk of such things as though everyone knows their meaning. The experience of the trenches and the sharing of that experience with his comrades was burnt into his consciousness.

The clarity with which these old men can recall their front-line experiences is startling and tragic; Gerald Denis [30] would like to forget but cannot. The violence and ferocity of war meant that men lived in a state of extreme tension, though for most of them it would be looked back upon as a high-point in their lives if only they could survive it unscathed.

NOTES

1. Pearson, R. Pte. 10/1180, Hull Commercials, 1915-1918. Diary. (Author's collection).
2. Ibid.
3. Graystone, J. W. Pte. 10/634, Hull Commercials, 1916. Diary. (Author's collection).
4. Ibid.
5. Pearson, R. Diary.
6. Graystone, J. W. Diary.
7. Weasenham, R. H. Pte. 11/682, 11th East Yorkshires, 1914-1917. Conversation with author, 1964.
8. Barker, A. Pte. 13th East Yorkshires, 1914-1918. Taped interview, 1988. (Author's collection).
9. Tait, J. Pte. 10/1281, Hull Commercials, 1915-1916. Malet Lambert Local History Originals, Vol. 8. (1982).
10. Pearson, R. Diary.
11. Slack, C. M. Lt. Grandfather's Adventures in the Great War. (A. H. Stockwell Ltd., 1977). p.117.
12. Ibid. p.57.
13. Ibid.
14. Beeken, J. L/Cpl. 10/695, Hull Commercials, 1914-1918. Diary. (Author's collection).
15. Graystone, J. W. Diary.
16. Tait, J.
17. Ibid.
18. Ibid.
19. Another name for these was Coal Boxes or Rum Jars.
20. Tait, J.
21. Slack, C. M. Grandfather's Adventures in the Great War. (A. H. Stockwell Ltd., 1977) p.58.
22. Weasenham, R. H.
23. Hilton, A. Sgt. 1/4th East Yorkshires, 1915. Diary. (Author's collection). His name is now inscribed on the Menin Gate.
24. Pearson, R.
25. Ibid.
26. Osborne, L. S. Bandsman, 11/341, 11th East Yorkshires, 1914-1918. Diary. (Author's collection).
27. Pearson, R. Diary.
28. Ibid.
29. Land, E. Pte. 11/648, 11th East Yorkshires. Taped interview 1989. (Author's collection).
30. Denis, G. K.R.R.C. 1915-1918. Taped interview, 1988. (Author's collection).

CHAPTER SEVEN

Mud, Blood and Bodies
The Somme,
1st July — 13th November, 1916

I T IS OFTEN SAID that the British campaign on the Somme was intended to ease the pressure on the hard-pressed French at Verdun, but by the end of June the German offensive at Verdun had stopped as the German army could not sustain such enormous losses. The preparations by the British may have helped to halt the Germans but now it was the British turn to take the offensive in the Somme Valley. Haig believed it was here a decisive victory would be won, though few of his entourage on the general staff shared this line of thought and Marshall Foch, the French commander, was most sceptical of Haig's plan. [1]

The Somme was unsuited to a British attack because the German troops occupied all the high ground; any attacking troops would have to fight their way uphill towards concealed defenders. The German defences here were neglected because there had never been any fighting in this area on any serious scale. As British activity increased the Germans began to strengthen their own positions and by 1st July the German front was massed with rows of fresh barbed wire and the first and second lines had become formidable positions with large dug-outs forty feet deep that could withstand the heaviest bombardments.

The battle of the Somme began as the British guns opened fire on an eighteen-mile front on 26th June. For six days the German front line was pounded with high explosive; the enemy lived for that time in deep dug-outs listening to the raging inferno above them and never knowing if the next shell would seal them and their comrades in a tomb, never again to see their loved ones. The walls of dug-outs rocked and concussion from the shells snuffed out candles and buffeted ears.

Freiwilliger Eversmann sat in his dug-out below Thiepval Ridge hoping for an end to this never-ending barrage:

"Shall I live till morning? Haven't we had enough of this frightful horror? Five days and nights now this hell concert has lasted. One's head is like

Troops waiting to move up the line, 1916

a madman's, the tongue sticks to the roof of the mouth. Almost nothing to eat and nothing to drink. No sleep. All contact with the outer world is cut off. No sign of life from home. How long is this going to last?'' [2]

The Pals of the 31st Division had been given what was supposedly the cushy part of the line because of their slight experience in trench warfare and absolute inexperience at attacking anything. Their brief spell in France had given them only a taste of trench life but it was now time for the real thing. The Hull Service Battalions had been in the line for over a week by 30th June and had been suffering the German retaliatory barrage all that time. Men were being used to carry equipment to the front and found themselves seconded to other units to help with the heavy work.

As the barrage roared around them and shells screamed overhead, Pte. Weasenham of the 11th remembers the fear they all felt and saw men shaking, tears rolling down the faces of some. [3] On the night of 30th June, parties were sent into no-man's-land as the barrage lifted. Pte. Carter of the Commercials felt intense relief to get out of his trench and do something useful. The enemy sent up showers of star-shells making no-man's-land as bright as day, the Hull men diving into shell holes whenever these burst. Slowly they made their way out to the German wire and to their horror found it virtually intact:

"In a few hours' time our chaps would be just strung upon it like washing. On our return to the front line we reported the matter, but I don't know that anything was or could be done about it at this late time." [4]

At 6.30 a.m. 1st July the British barrage increased all along the line, the whine and rumble of shells overhead became continuous and the explosions on the German line just added to the deafening noise. The Hull Pals were in the reserve trenches fully expecting to be called upon the participate in the coming battle. The small group of men who had been out in no-man's-land that night scrambled back into the front line but it was so packed they just slipped into holes in the trench side to keep out of the way until the attacking troops had gone over the top.

Ten minutes before zero hour a gigantic mine was exploded under Hawthorn Ridge and the ferocious barrage stopped. If the Germans were waiting for a warning that the British were coming, this was it. While British troops waited and their officers checked their watches the Germans scrambled out of their dug-outs and got busy setting up machine-gun positions and manning what was left of the trench system. Some of the Pals' Battalions had already left their trenches and lay out in no-man's land waiting for the order to advance.

At zero hour it was broad daylight. [5] At 7.30 a.m., on a bright and sunny morning, the whistles blew all along the front and the Pal's Battalions scrambled out into no-man's-land, formed up in long lines and began to walk towards the German line. The fate of these ill-used young men is well known: they were cut down in droves by the German machine-gunners who could

Troops fix bayonets as zero-hour approaches

not believe their eyes upon seeing men walking to destruction.

Pte. Pearson and his mates got out from their trench-side hideaways to watch the progress of the advance. At first they saw men walking in orderly line with rifles at the port; soon the machine-guns got to work and the lines of men became "just like falling stalks of corn." [6]

Over the top — the ultimate test for infantry, especially in broad daylight

A party of men from the Commercials had been attached to the Durham Light Infantry before the attack and had never been returned. Pearson saw them attack with the Durhams on his left and describes his feelings on seeing them annihilated:

> "Men whose names I remember even today. I felt like crying with fury that men's lives could be sacrificed so easily. This was just murder." [7]

During the morning Pte. Aust of the Commercials watched the survivors of a kilted battalion moving down a communication trench between the enemy's third and second lines:

> "On reaching the second line they spread out in what is called 'extended order' as though they were on the barrack square. The officer or NCO in charge rose and held up his arm. They all set off at a trot in perfect line towards our trenches. Within seconds a machine-gun was traversing them until the last man fell. I remember standing on the fire-step and screaming: 'Bastards, bastards'. That was a word I never used."

The main body of Hull Pals stayed in reserve all day and could get no news of what was happening, but rumours flew about and a feeling of helplessness came over the men:

> "We remained in reserve — feeling terribly depressed." [8]

When the afternoon came some men were detailed to carry ammunition to the front line but could not move very fast because all the communication trenches were packed with wounded and dying men who had got back to their own lines. Pte. Surfleet of the 13th was sent to fetch water that hot afternoon and records with dismay in his diary the terrible sight of the wounded blood-covered survivors of the attack, some limping, others being helped along by pals, "all with a look of indescribable fear in their eyes. I know now I hate this warring business." [9]

16 Platoon, D Company of the Hull Commercials were ordered to assemble at a certain trench in the early evening. They stumbled along the battered trench system that led to the rear. Pte. Aust was one of this party and never forgot the cries of the wounded, out in no-man's-land:

> "I have always been haunted by the voice of one, obviously delirious, who kept crying: Mother, mother!"

Later that day the Hull Commercials moved into the front line. They had been under fire now for over a week and had spent their rest time on working parties carrying supplies and ammunition to the forward positions: to say they were tired would be an understatement. The main fear now was that the Germans would take advantage of the situation and attack the line; there was little to stop them now. The company commanders decided to concentrate their men in the reserve line but asked for eight volunteers to man the front line and send up rockets in the event of a German attack:

> "To a man we had frightful headaches and had had so much concussion that we were all suffering from various degrees of shell shock." [10]

The men said nothing, only stood in silence that was broken as a shell exploded on the parapet knocking the helmet off one man. As no volunteers came forward the Captain in charge detailed eight bombers for the mission. At dusk they moved down what was left of the trenches to the front line:

"The last hundred yards was solid with men killed whilst waiting to go over. It was impossible to do other than walk on these bodies and I finally reached a man on a stretcher, with a bearer lying dead at each end. I raised my foot to place it on the chest of the man on the stretcher, when to my amazement, he popped his head up and said quietly, "mind my leg chum", and then just laid back again." [11]

Upon reaching the front a search had to be made for an inhabitable stretch of the line; rockets were set up and sentries posted and then the eight bombers settled down for what seemed the longest night of their lives. Later that same night the Hull Battalions were relieved.

Between the opening of the British barrage on 24th June, and the opening of the attack on 1st July, twenty-one men of the Hull Pals were killed by snipers or shelling. Another four died of wounds during the next four days. [12] The attack at Serre had been a total failure and although the Hull men had got off lightly, the 31st Division had suffered enormous losses.

Hull Pals men were sent to other units before July 1916. These three Hull men were killed attacking with the 11th East Lancs (Accrington Pals) at Serre on 1st July, 1916. Left: Cpl. Arthur Moore, son of Arthur and Norah Ann Moore of 62 Freehold Street, Hull. Died on his 21st birthday. Buried at Serre Road No. 2 cemetery. Centre: Cpl. W. C. Billington, age 26. Notice that this Hull man is wearing an East Yorks cap badge. Buried at Railway Hollow cemetery. Right: Pte. Clifford Lee, aged 28. Son of Harry and Ada Faith Lee of 88 Londesborough Street, Hull. Buried at Queens cemetery, Puisieux.

L/Cpl. Beeken of the Commercials recalls an atmosphere of gloom when out of the line, as many friends had been killed. [13] On the 2nd July Col. Pearson called together his officers and N.C.O.'s to give a talk on the first stage of the Somme battle, ending with the remark, "We would suffer many more casualties in this war but at the end of it all a 10th East Yorkshire Regiment would return to Hull, though you may not be there." Beeken pondered in his diary:

"We wondered what he meant to convey to us." [14]

The Battle of the Somme did not end on 1st July: several attacks were made in the summer, autumn and early winter. It was not until 18th November that it officially ended. For these four and a half months the Hull Brigade were constantly in and out of the line, a duty interspersed with trench raids and rest periods, though the latter usually meant working parties to carry out the never-ending fatigues. Then on the 12th November, 1916, they found themselves once more moving into the attack before Serre as the General Staff tried a last offensive on the Somme to win a victory and save face. The Germans were uneasy and knew something was afoot, but a major attack at this time of year and in these conditions seemed out of the question.

The night of the 12th was fine, cloudless and frosty as the troops packed tightly into the forward positions for the assault. The positions occupied between Serre and the Ancre on the 1st July were exactly the same only the season was different. The British artillery was pouring a withering barrage on the German line. As it paused from time to time, rifle fire could be heard in places from the Germans and the sharp crack of grenades exploding in no-man's-land. The assault troops could not return fire and risk bringing a German barrage on their tightly-packed positions. Shortly after midnight a thick fog gathered in the valley.

On the morning of the 13th the 10th (Hull Commercials) and the 11th East Yorkshires were kept in reserve and the 12th and 13th Battalions were to take part in the attack. Pte. Surfleet of the 13th remembers that morning as being dull, foggy and wet, the most thoroughly miserable day; everything was in a hopeless hubbub and bustle, even the mud seemed stickier and thicker. [15] This was, however, to be a lucky morning for Surfleet as men were required for a skeleton force to stay behind to form a core for new drafts coming in should the Battalion be destroyed. A coin was tossed to decide whether Surfleet or Bell should stay; Charles Bell lost and went off to his death. [16]

With heavy hearts the men remaining watched the Battalions prepare to attack:

> "There was an artifical air of jollity about . . . but it was the thinnest of veneers, a very feeble covering over the sense of grim reality which I felt the whole Battalion was feeling." [17]

At 6.45 a.m. the British barrage intensified on the German front line. On the left of the British line the 12th East Yorkshires and on the right the 13th East Yorkshires scrambled out into no-man's-land and advanced in four tightly-packed waves. The heavy fog kept it as dark as night as the bayonet men, bombers and lewis-gunners moved across the sodden muddy ground; the first wave passed snipers and lewis-gunners who had been sent into no-man's-land earlier to cover the attack. They were to join the fourth wave as it advanced.

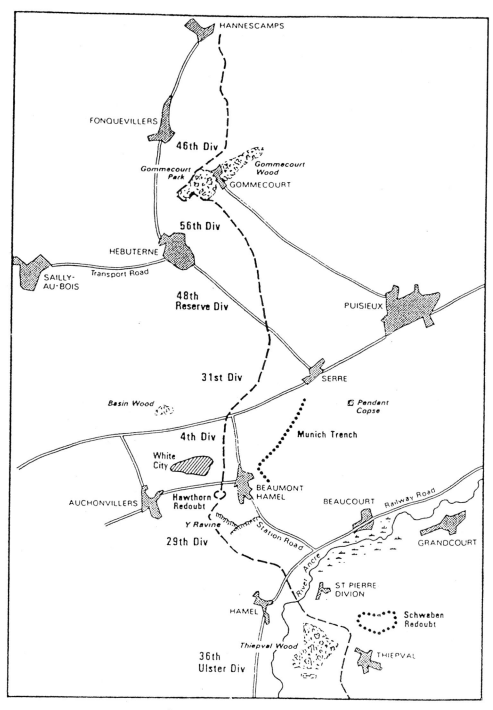

Serre, 13th November, 1916

The planned smoke screen had to be abandoned as the wind direction was unfavourable, but smoke was laid down by Engineers firing smoke bombs from mortars. The effects could not be judged as any aircraft observation was prevented by the heavy mist. This increased enormously the difficuly of maintaining communications with the attacking Battalions and made any accurate counter-artillery work impossible. Two tanks had been allocated to the Division to assist in the assault but could not operate due to the heavy state of the ground.

L/Cpl. Albert Barker, "D" Company, 13th Battalion, remembers men stuck in the mud before the German front line and being shot down before they could move. He dived for cover in a shell hole and found it full of men who had lost their rifles. Upon leaving he was hit to be taken prisoner later that day. [18] As the fourth wave left their trench still no enemy counter-barrage came down but Hebuterne was being heavily shelled. On the right of the Hull Battalions the 3rd Division was held up by heavy machine-gun fire and forced back to their own front line. This left the right flank of the Hull men unprotected.

The first wave entered the front line and prepared to hold it at all costs as the second, third and fourth waves passed over them in the mist. There was so little left of the German front line that some first-wave men walked over it without realizing. The Germans in the support trench put up a fierce fight and poured a withering fire into the ranks of the East Yorkshires. The support trench was finally taken, and any Germans found killed or taken prisoner. A plea was sent back for reinforcements but non came; the losses of the two attacking Battalions had been considerable. Capt. Watson of the 12th East Yorkshires returned to his own lines wounded with the following message:

> "We are holding the enemy second line but will have our work cut out to hold it without reinforcements." [19]

No reinforcements could get through as the Germans were by now putting down an inferno of high explosive on the British front line that made any forward movements impossible. The remnants of "D" Company that made up the fourth wave made their way to the German third line through rifle and machine-gun fire. Once in the trench flares were lit but could not be seen because of the fog and any communication with the rear was impossible as any runners sent were promptly captured. Capt. Wooley led the remainder of "D" Company into the abandoned third line and could find no one on either side of him for one hundred and fifty yards so he prepared to defend the captured trench.

The Germans could be seen forming left and right of the small band of Yorkshiremen, and were promptly shot if they showed themselves. They were too far way to use grenades but machine-gun and rifle fire soon began to harass the British attackers.

It would seem that Capt. Wooley and his small band had got through to the German third line by luck and had taken the Germans by surprise by being there at all. Wooley was a strict disciplinarian and believed his troops capable of anything; the men of "D" Company would have followed him anywhere and did. Outnumbered and surrounded, the doughty Captain even offered the Germans a chance to surrender which they refused. In the Captain's own words:

> "They were strong in numbers and stout fighters and refused to come."[20]

Twice the Germans attacked the position in squad formation but stuck in the mud and were shot down; snipers jumped from shell hole to shell hole but were killed before they could find a good position.

The attack in general had petered out during the morning and the British guns now began a heavy barrage on the German lines and on Capt. Wooley's position. At about 11 a.m. forty British prisoners were marched over open ground between the little outpost and the second line and this was repeated an hour later. In the afternoon the remnants of "D" Company were still fighting off the enemy with resoslution until roughly thirty British prisoners (Suffolks) were seen approaching; behind them were large numbers of German infantry. The defenders could not fire without killing their own men and between 3 p.m. and 3.30 p.m. the brave band defending were forced to surrender. Capt. Wooley and eight other ranks were taken prisoner. [21]

From 9.30 a.m. the German troops launched a series of resolute counter-attacks with bomb and bayonet, only to be repulsed time and again. By late afternoon the salient being held by the Hull Pals was the scene of continuous fighting as the two Battalions met with fierce opposition from the enemy. Many acts of bravery took place that day, often going unrecorded, though Pte. John Cunningham was to be awarded the Victoria Cross for conspicuous gallantry.

The situation became desperate as the officers commanding the operation became aware that even if the 12th and 13th East Yorkshires were reinforced, the effort would be wasted with their right flank totally exposed. The third Division must attack and hold the German front line. As the day drew to a close it became obvious that this was impossible and the position of the 31st Division untenable:

> "The only result of holding on would be that every available gun would be concentrated afresh on the narrow salient which we are now holding, in which case there would be a large sacrifice of life to no particular purpose." [22]

At 5.30 p.m. the order to withdraw was given, and the evacuation was completed by 9.30 p.m.

Back in the British lines the 10th and 11th Battalions were having a hellish time as the German barrage rained down upon them. "A" Company, 11th

JOHN CUNNINGHAM, V.C.
EAST YORKS. REGT.
H. Miles, Publisher, 23, Brook St.   Copyright.

Pte. John Cunningham, 13th East Yorks, won a V.C. before Serre,
13th November, 1916.

Battalion, was hard hit in the hail of high explosive. Pte. Osborne of "B" Company says little of that morning in his diary but his words have a familiar ring:

> "Wounded and dead in Home trench very thick, walking over dead bodies, Sgt. Walton killed, Sgts. Farey and Cox wounded." [23]

Rumours of gains began to filter back to the reserve positions but soon all became aware of the reality of the situation: yet another bloody failure. Surfleet was sent with thirty new arrivals to the front line later that afternoon. All they could do was to take out the dead and carry the wounded to the rear. Upon seeing the front line, Surfleet writes, "It was no longer a trench, it was a bloody ditch." [24]

The German shells continued to arrive at regular intervals as the wounded were taken to the rear and the sucking mud hampered the stretcher-bearers' work. Even when these men reached the dressing stations there was little relief. The doctors were worked off their feet and the place was packed with bleeding men; the whole place was penetrated by the sickly smell of iodoform and iodine:

> "The look on the faces of some of those lads down there made me hurry out into the fresh air, it was something not unlike the scene and smell of a slaughter house." [25]

As Surfleet and some of the new men trudged back to the front a shell burst among them, killing four and wounding a number of others. Once back at the front a call was made for men to go over the top; the men were at first reluctant but when they heard it was to bring in the wounded they all volunteered and went into no-man's-land in the darkness. The cries of the wounded and dying were terrible to hear:

> "It was awful to pass some of these men who shouted for us to take them back, but we had orders to leave anyone who could possibly get in on his own." [25]

The Germans were also taking in wounded and both parties could see each other but no shots were fired. Surfleet's small band came across a Tommy with both legs broken and a shattered elbow; he was lifted on to the stretcher and carried away. The little group got lost and it took them over two hours to get back. Surfleet went on ahead and found an R.A.M.C. post and to his amazement the stretcher-bearers refused to leave to get the wounded man. He thought their post "a bloody sight too safe and comfortable to be left." [25]

Surfleet went back to fetch his pals with their wounded comrade. They could not believe the response of the stretcher-bearers who, when they arrived, were sitting, smoking and drinking tea:

> "We handed our burden over to them — I can still feel my blood boil and still hear the flow of abuse we poured out to them, until, eventually they did put the lad on a trolley and set off with him to the dressing

station.'' [25]

When Surfleet's group returned late at night the Hull Battalions were being relieved and withdrew to their support position. Hot soup, tea and bread was served to the remnants of 12th and 13th Battalions (3rd and 4th Hull Pals). They were all falling asleep on their feet and after a heavy tot of rum slept a deep sleep. The next morning, when roll-call was taken, it became all too obvious that these Kitchener units would take part in no more attacks in 1916. On 13th November the collapse of the attack before Serre had been total and by mid-afternoon it was all over. Many of the Hull men who had gone over the top had become casualties and lay dead or wounded on the rising ground between the British and German trenches.

While in support, the 10th and 11th Battalions suffered casulaties from the barrage; in the 11th thirteen men were killed and in the 10th eight men were killed. In the 12th Battalion 139 men were killed and in the 13th 148 men were killed, with many more wounded or taken prisoner.

When being interviewed in 1988 about the 13th Battalion's part in the 13th November attack, Albert Barker was asked, ''What was it like on the Somme?'' He answered simply:

''Mud, blood and bodies.'' [26]

NOTES

1. Taylor, A.J.P. The 1st World War. (Penguin, 1987) p.130.
2. McDonald, L. Somme. (Papermac, 1986) p.49.
3. Weasenham, R. H. Pte. 11/682, 11th East Yorkshires, 1914-1917. Conversation with Author, 1966.
4. Pearson, R. Pte. 10/1180, Hull Commercials, 1915-1918. Diary. (Author's collection). During the barrage the 11th and 12th Battalions had sent out raiding parties but never got beyond the uncut wire.
5. A daylight attack was insisted upon by the French, in order to see the effects of their artillery.
6. Pearson, R. Diary.
7. Ibid.
8. Carter, Pte. Hull Commercials, 1916. Diary. (Author's collection).
9. Wilson, T. Myriad Faces of War. (Polity, 1986) p.354.
10. Middlebrook, M. The First Day on The Somme. (Penguin, 1984) p.240.
11. Ibid.
12. Soldiers Died in The Great War. Part 20. The East Yorkshire Regiment. (Haywood and Son, 1989) pp.57-75.
13. Beeken, J. L/Cpl. 10/685, Hull Commercials, 1914-1918. Diary. (Author's collection).
14. Ibid.
15. Wilson, T. The Myriad Faces of War. (Polity, 1986) p.355.
16. Bell, C. Pte. 14/213, 13th East Yorkshires. Enlisted Hull, 1914. Killed in Action, 13th November, 1916, at Serre.
17. Wilson, T. The Myriad Faces of War. (Polity, 1986) p.355.
18. Barker, A. L/Cpl. 13th East Yorkshires, 1914-1918. (Taped interview, 1988. Author's collection).
19. War Diary. H.Q. 92 Inf. B'de. 13th November, 1916. (Public Records Office, Kew.) 95/2356.
20. Wooley, Capt. 13th East Yorkshires, 1914-1918. Typed Statement. (Author's collection).
21. Ibid.
22. W.O. 95/41. (Public Records Office, Kew.)
23. Osborne, L. S. Bandsman, 11/341 11th East Yorkshires, 1914-1918. Diary. (Author's collection).
24. Wilson, T. The Myriad Faces of War. (Polity, 1986) p.355.
25. Ibid. p.356.
26. Barker, A. L/Cpl. Taped interview.

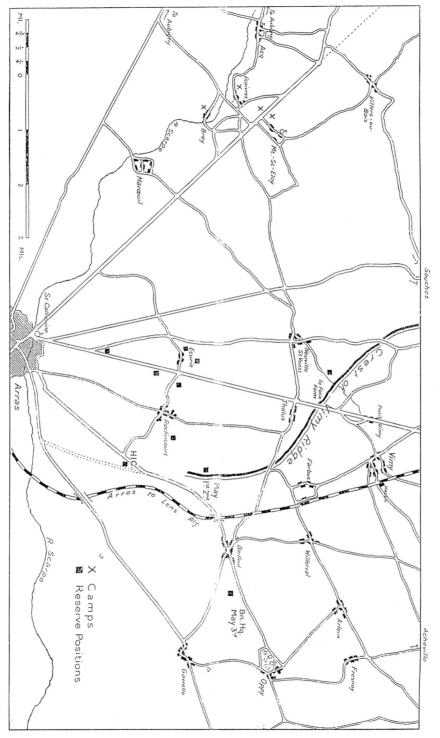

Oppy and Vimy Front, Back Areas, 1917

CHAPTER EIGHT

Hull's War,
Oppy Wood, 3rd May, 1917

T HE BATTLE OF ARRAS opened on April 9th, 1917. It was hoped yet again that the British Army would be able to deal the enemy a blow from which it could not recover and break through the deadlock in anticipation of a general advance.

A month earlier the German Army had withdrawn to the Hindenburg Line, a vastly superior defensive work that had been in preparation for many months. The withdrawal had begun on March 14th, leaving the British to advance through the devastated territory left behind. The Germans destroyed anything that might be of any possible use to the British: trees were cut down and booby traps left in plenty. The withdrawal shortened the German line by 26 miles and allowed ten divisions to be relieved of trench-holding duties:

> "The Battalion had a groggy time following up gerry over miles of evacuated mud and shell holes." (Sgt, Hull Commercials). [1]

When the British saw the enemy in retreat it was thought to be the downfall of German morale, but the hopes raised were to be dashed in the coming months.

The prelude to the attack was to be three weeks of wire cutting by Sappers and Infantry, followed by five days' bombardment by 2,879 guns, one to every nine yards. This, along with all the massive preparations that were visible to the enemy, gave away any hope of surprise. The Germans reinforced their troops and laboured night and day strengthening their new positions.

The battle opened with success for the attacking troops. Most of the German first line was captured and Vimy Ridge fell to the Canadians, but these victories were not extended due to stiff German resistance; the cavalry, massed at Arras to exploit the expected breakthrough, waiting for an order to advance that never came.

For a few hours there was hope of a breakthrough but the gamble had failed. No more could have been asked of the British troops; German resistance became obstinate and they launched a series of counter attacks, each one fiercer than the last. On April 14th the main phase of the offensive ground to a halt.

On April 16th, the French made a massed frontal assault on the Aisne and went forward to the same old slaughter. Haig decided to continue the offensive in order to assist the French advance, but by then there was no advance

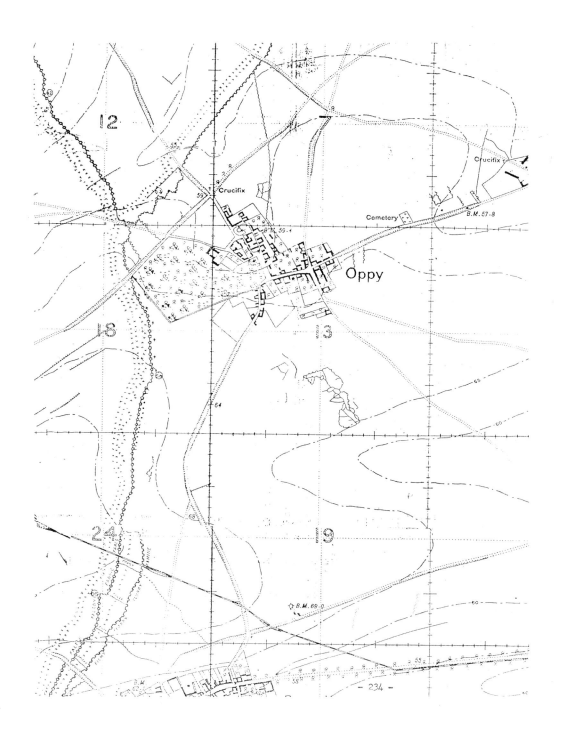

Oppy Trench Map, 1917

to assist. Still the British pressed forward at Guemappe and Gavrelle at an enormous cost in lives. By the end of April the French army was in a state of mutiny and unable to take part in the offensive but Haig decided to continue his own attacks and press forward towards a better defensive position. [2]

As the month of May opened the 92nd (Hull) Brigade were preparing to take their part in the Battle of Arras and on May 1st the 11th Battalion was resting in German dugouts that had been the old third line. That same afternoon a practice attack was made nearby over ground marked by white tapes. At 9 p.m. the next day the Hull unit left their billet between Roclincourt and Bailleul and marched to the assemble trenches facing Oppy Wood.

The Commercials moved forward on May 1st to trenches and gun pits near Maison de la Coté, overlooking Bailleul. Here they watched artillery duels, the British firing at Oppy Wood and the Germans at Bailleul:

> "Shells burst in the village (Bailleul) with the resultant clouds of brickdust, the colour intensified by the setting sun, providing a picture gripping in its awfulness." [3]

Soldiers taking part in all of this had little idea of being involved in anything of importance to anyone but themselves. When questioned about their experiences, their faces register pleasure that writers should be interested at all. What we see in retrospect as one event, like the Battle of Arras, the soldier was only aware of as his own personal experience and a fast-moving show of highlights interspersed with high tension and the fear of death, mutilation and hand-to-hand fighting. The journey through battle for the individual was a series of local actions and Pals' faces appearing and disappearing in the fog of war, thick smoke, isolation, terrific noise that few human voices could be heard through and the bursts of star shells adding an unreal lighting effect to the whole scene. All of this was burnt into the soldier's memory for the rest of his life.

The men of the Hull Brigade had experienced battle and knew what was in store for them in the forthcoming attack. Pte. Weasenham of the 11th felt a depression descend on him as he waited in the assembly trenches opposite Oppy Wood and wondered if he would ever see home and his young wife, Olive, again. He spoke of the comfort of having his pals around him but they all had little to say. Their mood was tense and grave, some carried a crucifix and sought solace in religion, last letters home had been written and money and jewellery pooled and so saved from the battlefield scroungers. The last night of safety was upon them; they formed into waves and waited in the darkness. [4]

In the German positions in and before Oppy Wood a Guards Division waited for the dawn. The Hull men had clearly been seen entering the line:

> "To get to the assembly positions Coys (Companies) had to go over the top of a rise within 1,000 yards of the Boche with a moon low in the sky behind them." [5]

As the 92nd Brigade formed up, Very lights went up on their western side and lit up the entire area. At 1.40 a.m. the Germans started an intense barrage on the British line which was to last more or less all day, fire so fierce the Hull men left their trenches and lay out in the open for two hours before zero hour.

The rear areas also received attention from the enemy artillery. Pte. Ernest Land was in the transport section of the 11th East Yorkshires and had tethered the horses in a wood. As he settled down for the night with his pals, shells began to explode in the wood. He rushed out from his tent and did not even have time to get his clothes on. With one leg in his trousers he leapt on to the nearest horse and, as shells screamed in, rode without a saddle hell-for-leather to safety. [6]

Just before 3.45 a.m. the men were back in position though the shelling had disorganised many companies in the ensuing confusion. To show yourself above the parapet was to court danger as the enemy were on the alert and constantly sniping, and bursts of machine-gun fire would open up without warning. L/Cpl. George Lewis Spring of the Commercials looked out into the darkness of no-man's land and was shot through the head. [7]

L/Cpl. George Lewis Spring, Hull Commercials. Killed just before the Oppy attack, 3rd May, 1917.

At 3.45 a.m. the British barrage opened up on the German front line:

> "As we checked our equipment in the dark our artillery opened up on Gerry. It was deafening and the ground shook beneath us." [8]

The enemy intensified their barrage and the result was " a chaos indescribable"[9] as clouds of smoke and dust added to the already poor visibility. The signal was given and the men of 92nd (Hull) Brigade advanced to the attack into the fire and blackness of no-man's-land. German machine-guns fired from the wood and from trenches before it and swept the whole front.

Pte. Green of "A" Company, Hull Commercials, went forward with the first wave and as he approached the German line found he was alone. He saw a group of twelve Germans in a machine-gun post and as it stopped firing threw in a hand grenade, killing four men and wounding one. The others threw up their hands and surrendered. Capt. J. C. Addy [10] then appeared on the scene telling Green to take them back: "You seem to have done your bit for the day." [11]. He took his prisoners to the rear, dropping the wounded man off at an advanced aid post.

Pte. Beeken of the Commercials remembers shells shrieking over him and bursting just in front, while German shells were bursting behind. As he walked forward the dead bodies of his comrades littered the ground:

"It was hell." [12]

The men were quite close to the wood but it could not be seen in the chaos, neither could the creeping barrage that they were supposed to follow. The terrific machine-gun fire brought the attack to a halt as men took cover in shell holes.

Different coloured Very lights over the enemy lines gave a surreal effect to the scene; Bill Smith of the Commercials said to Beeken as they advanced:

"Isn't it a pretty sight?" "Yes," he answered, "but isn't a lot of stuff missing us." [13]

Little contact had been made with the enemy, though parts of the first line were entered and groups of men began to lose their direction as the noise and darkness clouded their senses:

"The fumes almost choked us and I had a splitting headache." [14]

All they could do was walk towards the lights. Pte. Weasenham of the 11th advanced with "B" Company into a hail of machine-gun fire but could see no sign of the enemy through the fumes and darkness:

"I was hit in the arm and leg, as I lay there I could feel my pals falling on top of me, it was this that saved my life." [15]

Many years later he would describe himself as the luckiest man on earth whenever he spoke of Oppy. "B" Company of the 11th reformed their dwindling ranks three times in no-man's-land only to be driven back. Lt. Jack Harrison attacked a machine-gun single-handed, enabling his men to advance, and gave his life in the process. [16] "D" Company advanced, only to find the German wire intact; "C" Company entered Oppy Village but were surrounded and taken prisoner or killed. Even as daylight broke the attack had petered out. Many acts of heroism were performed before Oppy Wood, but to no avail. The same old tactics had forfeited any possibility of surprise

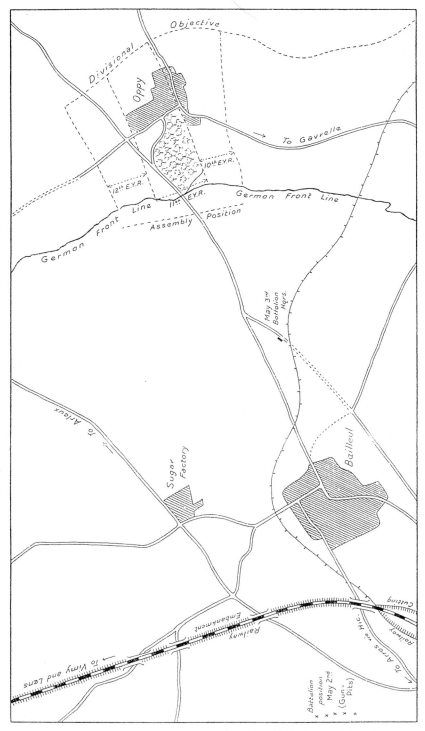

Oppy Attack, 3rd May, 1917 (Hull Pals positions)

and the Hull units had paid the price. All that remained now was to get back safely to their own lines.

At 5 a.m. Pte. Beeken met groups of men falling back and knew it was all over. Groups of German infantry were seen appearing from the smoke, though they retired quickly when fired upon. Many men in shell holes ran back through the barrage in a desperate attempt to escape and many more decided to lie low and wait for the night. The day was hot and sunny, aircraft of both sides flew overhead in the clear skies, the Germans sweeping the whole sector with machine-gun and artillery fire until darkness descended. Any men that were able returned to their assembly positions and stretcher-bearers went into no-man's-land to find wounded men and bring them in.

The 92nd (Hull) Brigade was relieved late at night and the survivors were marched alond the Lens-Arras road to a camp near Ecurie. They arrived about dawn, totally worn out by their experience and feeling very depressed at having suffered such casualties for nothing:

> "And even more so when we learned of the total casualties." [17]

In wartime dead comrades were forgotten with great speed, but directly after battle men would feel their loss sharply in the short rest period before returning to the line. The roll call was taken early on the 4th May. It was

Lt. Jack Harrison V.C., 11th East Yorks 1914-1917. He was a schoolteacher in Hull and a player for Hull Rugby Football Club. He won his V.C. at Oppy Wood. His body was never found.

a profoundly sad occasion as names were called out and not answered. The band were there to raise their spirits but the utter sadness of it all even affected the bandsmen who had not taken part but had lost many friends:

> "Band plays to broken down men, heart rending roll call. Where are the boys of the old brigade? Bandmaster plays 'End of a perfect day', with over half the battalion left behind us. Fond memories." [18]

As men resumed their duties and new men came into their ranks, post-battle depression was soon over. As they looked back on it all it was an experience of immense personal significance; they had seen and felt what few others had, and come out, if not unscathed, then alive. In years to come Pte. Weasenham would speak with other veterans in a very different way than with the rest of us. Those who emerged from the trial of battle were never the same again and any soldier who has experienced it will have a great affinity to others who have been through such a hell and lived to tell the tale.

The attack on Oppy Wood is built into the history of Hull and at Oppy a large stone monument exists to the men of Kingston upon Hull. [19] The local nature of the Hull Pals had become somewhat diluted after the Somme campaign and by May, 1917, it had practically gone, though quite a few originals still remained. The promise that 'men who enlisted together would serve together' was forgotten once on active service. Pearson describes men of the Commercials attacking with the Durhams on 1st July, 1916. Men were often removed from one unit to serve with another and the Hull Service Battalions were no exception.

As one example of casualty figures let us look at those given in the War Diary of the 11th Battalion, East Yorkshires, after the Oppy attack:

Capt. E. W. Reeve	)	Missing
2 Lieut. J. Harrison, M.C.	)	believed killed.
2 Lieut. W. R. Ekins	)	
2 Lieut. R. Woolcott	)	
Lieut. H. S. Staveley	)	Missing
Lieut. A. B. Hall	)	
2 Lieut. B. Hutchinson, M.C.	)	
2 Lieut. W. A. G. Purll	)	
2 Lieut. T. Burton	)	
2 Lieut. F. Davie	)	Wounded
2 Lieut. E. V. Galloway	)	
Capt. D. Barber	)	

9 O.R. Killed
150 O.R. Wounded
98 O.R. Missing

Total 257 O.R.

The total number of missing for each Battalion has often been taken for men killed; however a close look at <u>Soliders died in the Great War</u> [20] will show this to be inaccurate. The Hull Battalions were well below strength in May, 1917, the Commercials being only 550 strong and the 11th and 12th Battalions being not much better off. During the battle at Oppy Wood each unit lost 50 per cent of its men. But this included men wounded or taken prisoner. The deaths among other ranks according to the records are as follows:

10th Battalion — 69 dead
11th Battalion — 56 dead
12th Battalion — 81 dead
13th Battalion — 3 dead (in reserve)

Total 209

Reports in the past concerning soldiers killed at Oppy have tended to confuse the issue. On 5th May, 1977, the Hull Daily Mail reported 800 killed in the action and on 20th August, 1980, the same paper reported 2,000 men had died in the attack. However, of the 209 men that were killed on 3rd May, 1917, many had been brought into the East Yorkshires from other regiments such as the Northumberland Fusiliers, the Durham Light Infantry, etc. and had not enlisted at Hull. The numbers of Hull men killed in this battle were as follows:

10th Battalion — 39 dead
11th Battalion — 30 dead
12th Battalion — 29 dead
13th Battalion — 1 dead

Total — 99 [21]

Though the attack was a failure no more could have been asked of the Hull Service Battalions and we can only marvel that they launched attacks in the face of such opposition. The acts of bravery that day were too numerous to be counted and the majority will go unrecorded by historians. The men of the Hull Pals had a notion of duty that would seem out of place today, but their devotion and unswerving obedience and belief in the defeat of the German forces never faltered in the face of great adversity and sorrow. Let these men of Kitchener's Army be remembered for what they were, soldiers who were weary of war but never doubted that victory would come eventually.

NOTES

1. Hull Daily News. Peace Edition. 1919. p.16 (Author's collection).
2. Hart, B. L. History of the First World War. (Pan, 1972). p.321.
3. History of the 10th (Service) Battalion, East Yorkshire Regiment. (Brown and Sons, Hull, 1924) p.117.
4. Weasenham, R. H. Pte. 11/682, 11th East Yorkshires, 1914-1917. Conversation with author early 1960's.
5. War Diary. 11th East Yorkshires, May, 1917. (Prince of Wales Own Museum, York).
6. Land, E. Pte. 11/648, 11th East Yorkshires, 1914-1918. Taped interview, May, 1989. (Author's collection).
7. Spring, G. L. L/Cpl. 10/836, Hull Commercials. Lived at 712 Anlaby Road, Hull. Information given by his great nephew, Mr. Arthur Lewis Palethorpe, of Hull.
8. Weasenham, R. H. Conversation with author, 1962.
9. History of the 10th (Service) Battalion, East Yorkshire Regiment. (Brown and Sons, 1924) p.120.
10. Addy, C. D. Capt. Killed, Oppy Wood, 3rd May, 1917.
11. History of the 10th (Service) Battalion, East Yorkshire Regiment. (Brown and Sons, 1924) p.121.
12. Beeken, J. L/Cpl. 10/685, Hull Commercials, 1914-1918. Diary. (Author's collection).
13. Ibid.
14. Ibid.
15. Weasenham, R. H. Conversation with author, 1962.
16. Lt. Jack Harrison was awarded a posthumous Victoria Cross. He had worked in Hull as an Elementary School Teacher and was a popular member of the Hull Football Club, thrilling the crowds at the Boulevard with his dashing three-quarter play.
17. Pearson, R. Pte. 10/1180, Hull Commecials, 1915-1918. Diary. (Author's collection).
18. Osborne, L. S. 11th East Yorkshires, 1914-1918. Diary. (Author's collection).
19. The site for the memorial was given to the City of Hull by the Vicomte and Vicomtesse du Bouexic de la Drinnays. It was unveiled in 1927.
20. Soldiers died in the Great War. Part 20. The East Yorkshire Regiment. (Haywood and Son, 1989) pp.57-75.
21. Ibid.

CHAPTER NINE

Trench Raiding

T HE TRENCH RAID was devised in early 1915 to secure a prisoner and so gain intelliegence about enemy movements. There were also other reasons for such raids: they were intended to foster the men's fighting spirit and to make sure that the enemy could not relax. A raid moreover was valuable training for young officers whose daring and leadership had to be developed. The only problem was: could they survive this test?

Raids were planned at Head Quarters by staff officers who never took part and if a raid went wrong troops in the forward area would not feel kindly about these remote planners who deemed that the offensive mentality should be fostered just in case the front line got used to an easy life.

Word came to the Hull Commercials in June, 1916, that a trench raid was being planned to celebrate the King's official birthday. Pte. Pearson was not pleased at this prospect and wrote his thoughts down:

> "What a pity that the brass-hats who devised such things did not have to go and do it themselves, or at least take an active part in it." [1]

At the last moment the Commercials were deprived of this 'honour' and a detachment from the King's Own Scottish Borderers [2] given the task instead. Pearson watched the raiding party go by with blackened faces, all of them looking quite cheerful, but he confides in his diary:

> "I felt real sad for them." [3]

Officers in the Commercials though it might be a good idea to withdraw half of their men for a few hours to minimize casualty figures when the counter-barage came down, as the Germans knew something was afoot and were very nervous. Higher authority forbade this and "A" and "C" companies had to sit tight. [4] The raiders took no prisoners on that occasion but caused as much destruction as possible by bombing dug-outs and shelters. "A" and "C" companies, however, had to suffer a fierce counter-barrage that lasted for one hour and ten minutes, when nearly the whole trench line in that short front was blown in beyond recognition. A record of the chaos in the Commercials' trenches has been left us by an unnamed soldier:

> "I was in a bay with six men . . . a shell fell immediately behind the trench

> and two men were hit. One, 'Tich' West, was struck high up in the back,
> I placed him across my knee and was endeavouring to rip his tunic to find
> his field dressing when another shell blew in the parados burying us all.
> . . . I was buried in a kneeling positon holding a men I knew to be dead.''

The man lost track of time at this point; Sam Conyers tried to free him but
was killed, then his platoon sergeant tried and was badly wounded. Joe Allen
freed his head and a while after another man freed his arms and left him an
entrenching tool to dig himself out. At this point the man became light headed
and started singing and telling his leg he would not go without it. An officer
digging men out told him to shut up or the Germans would come over. [5]

> "At least five of the lads who had joined around the time I joined and
> had trained with me and lived in the same hut at Hornsea were killed and
> others seriously wounded." [6]

The raid went on record as a resounding success and the men who took
part went off for a well-earned rest, leaving the Hull men to pick up the pieces,
bury their dead and repair the badly damaged trenches, the working parties
labouring many hours after the raid to complete their work.

As the war progressed, raids became more and more elaborate and would
be planned with great attention to detail. Bombardments would open up as
the attackers went over the top and so gave the advantage of surprise. All
men would dress as Privates and no identification, civilian or military, would
be carried. Faces and hands would be blackened and some would wear
balaclavas. Metal would be tarnished and specialist weapons that had evolved
for close-quarter fighting would be carried. These would include knives, home-
made spiked clubs, shortened bayonets and hand-grenades. Some kind of
marking would at times be placed on the backs of the attacking troops so
they could tell their comrades from enemy troops in the confusion of the
melée.

As an example of a particularly daring type of raid let us study in detail
a raid made by 11th Battalion, East Yorkshires (2nd Hull Pals), on 8th
November, 1917. The raid was well rehearsed behind the lines on 4th, 5th,
6th and 7th November and when the day came each man was thoroughly
briefed as to his own particular role. Taking part were 13 officers, 406 other
ranks and 16 sappers from 223 Company, Royal Engineers, to carry out the
demolition work. The aim of the raid was to capture prisoners and to blow
up enemy dug-outs.

At 12 noon on the 8th November artillery, mortars and a large number of
Vickers machine-guns opened up on the enemy; at the same time the Hull
men moved forward before Fresnoy village and entered the German front
line. One unusual aspect of this raid was the use of dummy gas; this was only
yellow smoke projected by artillery but the sight of this yellow cloud was
enough to cause panic among the defenders. Gas helmets were put on and
the majority of them were still in their dug-outs when the attackers arrived.

In the German front line 54 enemy troops were killed and 21 taken prisoner for intelligence purposes. Many of the defenders tried to make a break for it from Fresnoy trench but were cut down by artillery, machine-gun and rifle fire. The Germans still in dug-outs in Fresnoy trench were told to come out but refused as they believed the gas to be real; they and the dug-outs were blown up with 20 pound mobile charges. It is estimated in the 11th Battalion's War Diary that at least 150 were killed in this way. [7]

At 12.20 p.m. the withdrawal back to the British front line began. The 11th Battalion suffered casualties of 5 officers and 52 other ranks, compared to at least 200 Germans killed, 21 prisoners taken and much enemy equipment destroyed. This was considered to be a great success, and the raiders spent the next day at Mont St. Eloy cleaning up and resting.

Not all raids were as successful as this and it seems the unusual ploy of using dummy gas was what made it outstanding in its results. Indeed, as raids became more frequent the more prepared was the enemy, so future raids would become more risky. Trench raids were yet one more drain on the Hull units' manpower, while the value of such activities was limited and did nothing at all to break the deadlock on the Western Front. In a raid in 1916 Lieut. Cecil Slack, 1/4th East Yorkshires, learned how a lack of co-ordination between the attackers and the artillery in the rear could bring about failure. Slack's men were approaching the German line when shells began to fall short among the Yorkshiremen and few of them managed to reach their objective:

"Our shells had done for us." [8]

Trench raids were a regular experience for troops at the front and were often bloody affairs, sparking off counter-raids by the enemy, mounted so as not to give the other side the upper hand in this form of warfare. And so it went on, with raid followed by counter-raid, each one more carefully planned than the one before, until by 1918 both sides had perfected their technique to a high degree. But when the German Army was to break the deadlock in March, 1918, it was to prove catastrophic to the army in retreat as they knew nothing but how to hold a trench and how to make the occasional sally across no-man's-land. All of this was to change shortly and the skills of a war of movement would have to be learned by these hardy subterranean dwellers of the front.

NOTES

1. Pearson, R. Pte. 10/1180, Hull Commercials, 1915-1918. <u>Diary.</u> (Author's collection).
2. This is incorrect. The East Lancashires carried out the raid.
3. Pearson, R. <u>Diary.</u>
4. A History of the 10th (Service) Battalion, East Yorkshire Regiment. (Hull Commercials). (Brown and Sons, Hull, 1924) p.77.
5. <u>Ibid.</u>
6. Pearson, R. <u>Diary.</u>
7. <u>War Diary.</u> 11th Battalion, East Yorkshire Regiment. 8th November, 1917. (Prince of Wales Museum, York).
8. Slack, C. M. <u>Grandfather's Adventures in the Great War.</u> 1914 to 1918. (Stockwell Ltd., 1977) p.68.

CHAPTER TEN

The Great Retreat, March 1918

MARCH OF 1918 saw the great allied armies on the Western Front in a state of near-total exhaustion. The French were a fragile entity after the mutinies of 1917 and it was not known for sure if they would hold a German attack. The British army had seen nearly all of its divisions involved in murderous offensives in 1917; the engagements of Arras, Third Ypres and Cambrai had taken a terrible toll in lives and left units badly depleted. The Russian army had just capitulated and after the signing of the Peace Treaty at Brest-Litovsk, large numbers of German troops had become available to replenish their forces on the Western Front.

Reinforcements for the British Front line had begun to dwindle and the whole army was reorganized, with each brigade now consisting of only three battalions instead of four. The 12th and 13th East Yorkshires were disbanded, leaving only two Hull battalions, and the spare men were used to bring the 10th and 11th battalions up to strength. Men such as Pte. Surfleet left the army and transferred to the Royal Flying Corps. The 92nd Brigade now consisted

Henry Hilyard of York, killed while serving with the Hull Commercials near Laventie, April 1918

of the following elements:

>10th East Yorkshires (Hull Commercials)
>11th East Yorkshires (2nd Hull Pals)
>11th East Lancashires (Accrington Pals)

These units now contained a fair number of conscripts, since voluntary recruitment could not possibly fill the ranks fast enough to keep up with the continual wastage of life at the front. Medical standards were lowered and men who were once turned down were now allowed to join up. Henry Hilyard of York was found medically unfit for military service on 10th December, 1915. He was drafted in at a later date to the Northumberland Fusiliers, transferred to the Hull Commercials and killed in the fighting near Laventie in 1918. [1]

The feeling among the troops was now far different from the early days of the war. 1916 and 1917 had seen many British offensives and a massive loss of life. The men were weary after two years of attacking the German lines only to be thrown back with heavy casualties and many wanted to see an end to it all. L/Cpl. Spencer wrote:

>"I trust this year will be one more favourable to us than the last was and that in its early path we shall see an end of the slaughter." [2]

But even though they felt a lack in confidence towards their leaders the will to win prevailed above all else, as Spencer testified:

>"We have been fooled and betrayed but yet we are confident of the outcome and be it soon or late victory will be ours." [3]

The men had faith in each other and in the officers that led them and this, combined with a belief that victory would come eventually, bound them together into a tight-knit fighting force. Though their numbers were badly depleted the British forces entered 1918 somewhat shabby but unbroken in spirit. This was to hold them together in the coming German offensive.

Ludendorf had chosen to make his first strike against the Southern part of the British sector. On his left his forces would be attacking Gough's Fifth Army but it was to the north of Fifth Army's front that Ludendorf pinned his hopes, the area between Arras and the Flesquières Salient, which marked the boundary between the Fifth and Third Armies. It was his intention to defeat the British forces in 1918, in the belief that French resistance would then collapse and that American intervention, on any scale, would make no difference.

The storm broke on the 21st March at 4.30 a.m. 750,000 German troops advanced and overran the Fifth Army. The British troops in this sector numbered only 300,000 and before the end of March the Germans would advance forty miles. The German troops were now using new tactics. Gone were the days of long lines of men walking forward. They relied on surprise, a concentrated but short-lived artillery bombardment and infiltration. For the latter the attacking troops would have going before them units of storm-

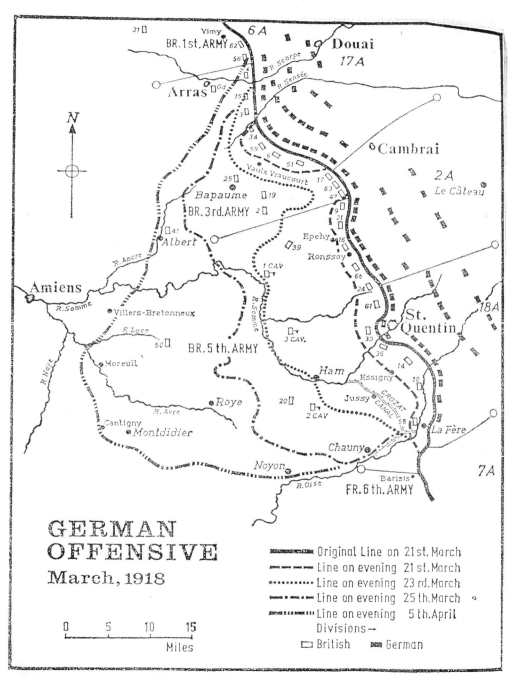

German Offensive, March, 1918

troopers, whose function was to advance where resistance had crumbled and by-pass any strong points still holding out, which would be eliminated by the follow-up forces. The main aim of the new storm-troops was to advance quickly, overrun the enemy artillery and strike at the support systems of the front-line men.

On March 20th, the 11th East Yorkshires were at La-Thieloye with the 10th East Yorkshires at Monchy Breton, both units looking forward to a well-earned rest. Sports events of all kinds took place and the troops were entertained by the Battalion concert party under their new name 'The Joy Birds'. Inoculations were given to the men of the 11th Battalion and they were promised the next day in bed to recover.

Men of the 12th East Yorks have their feet inspected for 'trench foot' by the M.O., near Roclincourt

The short 'History of the 11th East Yorkshires', published in 1921 in Hull, offers only a very brief outline of events between 21st and 27th March. Little detail is offered and the overall impression given is one of a unit in perfect working order and moving as one. The accounts left in diaries, however, are more human and truthful as to developments between the dates mentioned. Let us follow the paths of three individuals that were involved in their own fight for survival: one from 10th East Yorkshires, one from the 11th East

Yorkshires and one from the 1/4th East Yorkshires.

First comes an account left us by 11/341 Louis Stephenson Osborne, Bandsman, "B" Company, 11th East Yorkshires. On 21st March, 1918, at 3 a.m.,"B" Company were got out of bed and ordered to pack at once in readiness to move off. Osborne's arm was still sore from his inoculation and he felt sick and dizzy. Fatigues were carried out and a breakfast of sorts had by the men. The Battalion set off and went some way along the St. Pol Road before halting and falling out at the roadside. Lines of London omnibuses waited to take the troops to their destination, and rumours began to fly as the men speculated as to their prospects for the future:

> "War over, off back to Blighty — off to Ypres, next minute Armentières, again back to Somme, going to Turkey. Where the devil are we going?"

Osborne sat in the darkness feeling very ill, hungry and fed-up:

> "Far from home, aching arm, fat-headed, lay on roadside blissfully indifferent and with not the slightest interest."

The sounds of shells bursting on St. Pol could be heard clearly and Osborne commented "looks like the war is just commencing". He had no idea how close he was to the truth, as this was the opening barrage of the German offensive. Orders and counter-orders arrived at the Battalion H.Q.; the men boarded the buses but sat for another hour before moving off in the direction of St. Pol where shells were falling. The men continued to speculate as to their final destination.

As the buses were held up because of the barrage on St. Pol, Osborne and his pals listened intently for the next incoming shell. He describes them all as having the "wind up very much". One landed in the vicinity and at last the buses moved out of St. Pol as shells straddled the area.

*Bandsman Lewis Stephenson
Osborne, 11th East Yorks
1914-1918*

The buses moved on to Doullens while rumours circulated among the confused tommies, and as they left Doullers the troops were taken past a cemetery where the burial parties were already busy burying bodies as fast as they could:

"Blessed are the departed I wonder when we shall depart . . . Looks very uninviting round here."

As Osborne and his pals left their transport long lines of ambulances and walking wounded were seen heading for the casualty clearing station at Doullens. The troops marched to a nearby village and were put into billets:

"And told to make our miserable selves 'appy".

At 8.30 p.m. a meal of dry bread, watery soup and tea was handed out and the men tried to get some sleep laying on groundsheets with greatcoats for blankets. Shells continued to fall round about. After a short period of time an N.C.O. barked out the order, "Fall in immediately, fighting order"; the men's tempers flared as they were disturbed yet again:

"What a row, cursing and swearing, everyone goes mad. All shouting and bawling, no-one knows why."

The sorely-tried men fell in outside to find the streets packed with British troops. Col. Gurney addressed the men and told them:

"The next few days will tell on us all who live to come through it, the Germans have broken through and are driving us back."

Osborne's company set out just after midnight to an unknown destination. As they foot-slogged through the darkness the devastation was apparent to them all. Fires lit up the night sky and shells screamed by on all sides. When the men halted for a few minutes' rest they would go straight to sleep only to be revived to continue their grim journey. When daylight broke the men found themselves at Ervillers and were now part of the Third Army.

The scene that greeted the Hull units was one of chaos and carnage. The Y.M.C.A. was deserted but fully stocked, camps were abandoned and hospitals evacuated. Dead and wounded lay on the ground and shells exploded round about. Everything was in a terrible muddle and the officers were cursing and raving. The men lay down at the road side and tried to get some sleep, but the shelling was so heavy they were forced to move on:

"Weary and forlorn, fed up and hopeless, drag our weary selves along a road, no object in view, no formation, all in groups over all the road."

The shells continued to fall about them as the men wandered aimlessly among burning deserted camps. The Y.M.C.A. and the Quarter Masters' stores were looted for a few luxuries. They might as well have them as leave them to the Germans:

"The roads are strewn with dead men, some horribly multilated, we look

German troops move forward for the March Offensive, 1918

German troops mass behind the front and await the move into the line.
March 1918.

at some and pass on unheeding, wondering whether we shall be next. Here
a man's leg and thigh, there an arm, again a mutilated mule, blood drenches
the roads."

The men eventually arrived back at Ervillers after walking in a circle; orders
came and they dug in before an abandoned British camp and were told to
hold on at all costs. The work was hard but by midnight a deep enough trench
had been dug to allow the troops to rest; each man received a mug of tea
and settled down to get what sleep he could. The night was black and not
a sound was to be heard. Osborne thought the silence ominous. The anticipated
direction of the enemy was uphill from the defenders though the position
of the German troops was not known for sure. "B" Company were dug in
on either side of a main road with Osborne, his brother Stanley and Lt. James
holding the first post on the right.

As the Hull men sat and waited in the darkness a heartrending scream broke
the silence. This was followed by loud moans at intervals indicating the pain-
fully slow progress of a wounded German soldier towards the British lines:

"His groans turn one's blood cold."

When first light was to break this man was found dead at the roadside. In
the night Lewis and Stanley Osborne were ordered to search the camp to their
rear. They searched each hut in turn but were very glad to find nothing:

"Very dark. Wind up very much."

With the job done they both felt relief at returning safely to their own lines.
The night passed slowly as the men, exhausted from lack of sleep and
sustenance, watched and waited. To their front the Scots Guards held a thin
line some two hundred yards away. With the break of dawn came the German
barrage and shell after shell exploded around and among "B" Company. All
morning the barrage rained down on them killing and maiming many. Shouts
of 'stretcher bearer' filled the air but none were availble:

"We helpless stand and look on and see our own men fall time after time."

The noise of explosions was tremendous. German aircraft came over the
area and dropped bombs. The German artillery raised its sights and sent shells
into the camp in the rear; as each hut was hit it crumbled like matchwood.
All the while Osborne was under a constant hail of shrapnel and debris:

"Our thin line weakens considerably. Day wanes on without food or rest."

Lt. James and Stanley Osborne crawled to the top of the forward slope to
see if there was any enemy movement. The officer commanding the Scots
Guards said he would hold on to the last but his men were very demoralized.
When Lt. James and Stanley Osborne returned, they reported that they had
seen massed German assault troops preparing to move forward. The order
was given to 'stand to' at once:

"The haggard worn look on the men's faces is very disheartening, tears

Small crack units of German storm troops move to the attack with rifles slung and stick-grenades in hand.

The morning of 21st March, 1918. The main body of the Germany army attacks.

> of desperation roll down their cheeks, but determined to hold on we make
> a gallant stand to.''

News arrived that gave the men a boost. Col. Gurney told them they were
to be relieved by the French the next day. Taking new heart the troops stood
at their posts:

> "Suddenly a terrific screaming and roaring rends the air. Horrible coarse
> oaths and language, my hair stands on end.''

The Scots Guards rushed towards the line held by the East Yorshires, totally
panic stricken:

> "For God's sake fly, they shout, go like hell, they're on us, thousands and
> thousands of them, we have no chance whatever. For God's sake turn and
> run.''

The order ran down the line: "Hold fast East Yorkshires, hold them in check
and make them reinforce you.'' But they could not be stopped, leaving the
remnants of the 11th Battalion with only the enemy before them and no support in the rear. Osborne could see clearly the German infantry with their
transport advancing down the farther slope beyond the valley, yet no attempt
was made to attack the British line:

> "White drawn faces, bolting eyes, knocking knees and faulty step, nerves
> strained to the utmost was the prevailing feeling in our line.''

The men just wished the Germans would come and get it over with, but the
fall of the night put a stop to any more large-scale manoeuvres by the enemy
and the German guns fell silent as snow began to fall. The Hull unit had been
outflanked by the enemy during the night and the order came down to retire.
With bayonets fixed the men left those bloody trenches, passing posts where
many of their pals lay dead. With hindsight it is known to have been a narrow escape, as the Germans had advanced in a horseshoe around them and
they only got out as the gap was about to be closed.

On the immediate left of the Hull unit there was great activity and a fierce
bombardment raged. On they marched away from the enemy; the weather
was very cold and sleet began to fall. The 11th Battalion fell out at the roadside hoping to get some sleep, but after a while the men woke up frozen stiff
and continued their march to the rear. When daylight broke the men retreated
through a scene of carnage; only hours previously this spot had been the scene
of a fierce fight. Dead lay all around and wounded men were dying unattended:

> "In the grey light of dawn it was an awful picture and the mystery was
> where could the Germans be?''

Judging by the direction they had come from, Osborne thought it impossible
that the Germans could be anywhere near them, but the fighting in this area
had been very severe. The Germans were in fact snapping at the heels of the
Yorkshiremen and though their advance had been slowest against the Third
Army it had not yet run out of steam.

In the early morning of March 26th the men were ordered to dig in along the bank of a sunken road on front of Ayette. Lt. James shared oxo cubes with the Osborne brothers and rations were brought up for the first time since leaving La-Thieuloye. After a breakfast of dry bread and cold bacon they began to fortify their new positions; to the front nothing had yet appeared on the sky line and just near the newly-dug trenches was a stock of shells that was too close for comfort. The men began to remove them to a safe distance but before this task could be completed newly-sited German machine-guns opened up all along the sunken road, forcing the men to return to their trenches:

> "Another long weary day passed, nothing happening except Jerrie's ceaseless machine-gun fire and artillery shelling."

Just behind the East Yorkshires position and about 800 yards in front of Ayette stood an abandoned aerodrome, which was shelled constantly throughout the day and the following night. Outposts were manned as darkness fell but shortly afterwards the pickets were all killed. Anxiously the men looked for reinforcements but none came and the story of their relief by the French was seen to be only a myth. Not a shot had been fired by the British artillery as they had retired and were busy taking up their new positions.

Two more patrol parties were sent out but no-one returned. Capt. Southern of "B" Company needed scouts and patrols to find out what he could about any enemy movements and to find out how close they were. Lt. James and Sgt. Heedler went out but ten minutes later Lt. James returned as the Sergeant had been killed. Pickets were thrown out once more, Lt. James and the Osborne brothers crawled out in the darkness to man one post, machine-gun bullets whizzing around them as they crawled half-way up a slope and began to dig in. Just before daybreak a hole large enough to hold the three men had been dug and as the hours of darkness ran out they camouflaged their work. One post neglected to do this and invited the attentions of the enemy artillery and machine-gunners; they were all killed:

> "By daylight, Lt. James, Stan and I occupy our little trench, sat with our knees under our chins. We manage to have a scratch meal with the aid of a Tommie's cooker."

The three men could not move or stand up without giving away their position; there they sat numb, cold and desperate with only the rum to keep them going. Enemy aircraft came over and dropped bombs and the enemy barrage increased as high-explosive rained down upon the beleaguered troops. Still they dared not move as the bombardment grew heavier and earth and shrapnel began to fill their little trench:

> "Each moment looked like our last. Lt. James asks us to say our prayers. We all shake hands and bid each other farewell. Three unkempt, unshaven beings, tired, hungry and cold with bolting eyes, sat waiting for the end which seemed inevitable. I looked as Stan's face, the horror stricken look, then at Lt. James' also grey and ashen, mine felt the same."

Still they sat stiff with cramp, with shells falling about them faster than ever. Osborne became desperate and wanted to leave his post. He could see nothing around him for smoke and fumes and expected to be overrun by the enemy or killed by shells. At about mid-day a feeling of unreality came over him and his mind began to wander:

> "We grew oblivious to what was happening, only sat and wondered how long we should last. Home seemed like a dream we had had some far off time ago. The barrage fell all around us, shrapnel rained on us, yet we seemed fated to be unhurt."

Early that afternoon the barrage lifted from their positions and a voice shouted out: "They're coming". What was left of the Battalion scrambled out of their makeshift trenches and rushed up the hillside. As Osborne left his trench he felt something strike him hard in the back but turning round saw nothing and went to join his comrades now forming a thin line to make a stand. The sight that greeted them was of hundreds of field-grey clad infantry moving quickly down a hill towards them. Osborne fell to the ground as the Battalion opened a rapid fire into the attacking troops. Upon trying to open the breech of his rifle he felt a searing pain in his chest and back; looking down he saw his tunic was saturated with his own blood. His brother Stanley bound his wounds and sent him off to find a dressing station as the battle raged all around them. Lewis Osborne had been hit in the chest by a bullet that had passed clean through him.

As he trudged back to the sunken road, Osborne was in a terrible state, blood was pouring from his wounds, nose, ears and mouth. Wanting only to rest he fell into a trench but was brought round by an exploding shell and staggered on through the aerodrome to the dressing station at Ayette. There was nobody to attend to Osborne's wounds and he was told the staff there were packed and about to retire; one man told him to start for Courcelles aerodrome some distance away. Osborne struggled on, doubled with pain, completely exhausted and still bleeding profusely. Desperation drove him on and still the shells fell about him. He managed to reach Courcelles and staggered into the casualty clearing station to be told to lie on a bed without a mattress, the wires sticking into the open wound in his back. Osborne lay there waiting for an ambulance but instead he was told to leave as the Germans were advancing with great speed. He stepped outside to find the roads blocked with retreating British troops.

Osborne's strength was by now failing him fast as he staggered along a road packed with artillery and troops:

> "Several shells burst nearby, the mules take fright, everything is bedlam."

One artilleryman, seeing his plight, helped Osborne along the road and guided him away from the mass of limbers and guns. At the roadside he was propped against a tree given chocolate and biscuits by his helper who told him to get along after a rest. Osborne's retreat ended here. When he awoke he was on a cold table-top being attended to by a hard-pressed sister in a hospital. From here he went to Doullens casualty clearing station and then to No. 5 General, Rouen, and then home to England.

Osborne grumbled and moaned as events gathered pace at the start of the offensive but he had a lot to complain about. The lack of sleep, lack of food and the constant marching took its toll on the whole unit as they moved toward the enemy. The constant shell-fire nearly broke them as the Germans poured a fierce barrage upon the British lines. The exact position of the enemy was not clear and when they were at last spotted they were in great numbers compared to the thin khaki line of East Yorkshires.

Osborne describes part of a Guards unit running away from the enemy at one point. This is not a common event but unless there is a complete rout nothing would be made of it. Osborne's Battalion was driven back to Ayette where it made a last stand. Even after all the men had been through, when the order came to turn and fight not a man neglected his duty and after seven days marching and fighting the German army was stopped in its tracks. The British units around Ayette had suffered tremendous losses, but they had inflicted even greater losses on the enemy and Ludendorf could not afford to lose so many of his troops.

Let us now turn to the 10th Battalion, or Hull Commercials. This account of the retreat has been left by 10/1180, Pte. Reginald Pearson, who was a stretcher bearer.

The Commercials paraded at 7.30 a.m. on the morning of 22nd March, 1918. News of the German attack had not reached them until midnight on the 21st, though they could hear gunfire and shells falling on St. Pol all that day. Not much attention was paid to this and the men played company football as the battle raged on the Third Army front. When the whole Battalion was assembled they were marched through La Thieuloye where the 11th had been billeted and boarded London omnibuses on the main Arras — St. Pol road. At 10.30 a.m. they set off and passed through St. Pol and Doullens, stopping nine miles from Arras where they debussed and marched to Bailleulmont.

Here pay was issued, which seemed odd. Men going into battle had little use for money. Very heavy firing could be heard up the line and rumours began to fly as to how far the Germans had advanced. The Battalion was ordered to be prepared to move at short notice and a few men from each company were taken to the Quarter Master's Stores to be used as reinforcements later:

"The inevitable prelude to battle."

A fierce barrage was falling on the front lines as Pearson's company marched off at 8.30 p.m. The destruction of war was everywere: houses were ruined, trees uprooted and burning buildings lit up the night sky:

"By now many of us were asleep on our feet."

They marched all that night and at 6 a.m., as daylight broke, reached a sunken road near Hamel-Court. [5] It was bitterly cold but the men were so tired they lay down at the road-side to sleep until woken by the terrific noise of a bombardment not far away. The Commercials then went in reserve just west of Ervillers with the 11th East Yorkshires and the 11th East Lancashires to their front.

Pte. Reginald H. Pearson, 10th East Yorks 1915-1918

Orders came later that night to withdraw and Pearson's company moved back in good order and dug in just in front of a railway embankment:

"We prepared to await the coming of the enemy. I had just found a quiet corner to get my head down for a sleep when the order came to retire."

The enemy continued to advance on the right and so the men proceeded to retreat through an arch of a railway embankment. Pearson was walking with a mate from Goole and looked back towards the enemy when:

"There was this funny sound and a startled cry. Looking at him I saw him clutching his face and blood coming through his fingers."

He drew the man off the road and behind the shelter of a garden wall to examine his wound. A bullet had passed through both cheeks, smashed his teeth but fortunately missed his tongue. Pearson was worried in case the Germans should overtake them so he quickly plugged the bullet holes with cotton-wool after getting his friend to swill his mouth out with water. Both men set off across open country in search of a first-aid post. One was found not far away and he left the man there and set off in search of his unit.

As he walked along Pearson wandered in front of a well-camouflaged battery of 18 pounders as they were about to open fire:

> "When they suddenly all fired they nearly blew my head off."

Further on he came across one of the Battalion stretcher-bearers and teamed up with him. In late afternoon they found Brigade Headquarters and were given a meal and a night's rest. The next morning he set off once more in search of his unit:

> "Events now, such as times and places, became somewhat vague because there were so many and so fast."

He found "D" Company dug in on the edge of the aerodrome at Courcelles and commenced to enlarge his own bit of trench to accommodate his kit. Hardly had he settled down when the shout went up for a stretcher-bearer. In front of the next slit-trench a man was lying wounded out in the open. Pearson grabbed his bag of dressings and crawled over to the next trench. He was at once spotted by the enemy and machine-gun bullets whistled over his head. Once in the next trench he looked over the top and saw where the wounded man was. Keeping as near to the ground as possible he crawled out thirty yards to find a bullet had smashed the man's thigh. All the time a constant hail of machine-gun fire was being kept up. It would have been suicide to stand up, so Pearson had to think of another way to get him back:

> "Using his rifle and good leg as splints I bound them both together, crept in front of him with my legs opened in a v-formation, told him to crawl up between them and haul himself forward by taking hold of my belt and then, half on top of me, I dragged him back to the trench."

Here the splint fastenings were completed and the man set off to an aid post with two other stretcher-bearers. By now enemy trench-mortars had joined in with the machine-guns and the order came to retire again.

By the time Pearson had collected his gear and stretcher, "D" Company had gone. He set off after them but had to stop to catch his breath after his exertions. After going only yards he came across a wounded man from the East Lancashires lying on the road. His hip was shattered and he looked at Pearson hoping to be helped but said nothing:

> "His own unit must have left him but I just could not, even though I did not know what to do to help him single-handed."

The man was helpless and far too heavy for one man to carry. Behind a hut Pearson saw a wheel-barrow and throwing away his stretcher brought it to the wounded soldier and manhandled him onto it:

> "He never even murmured a word of pain or reproach."

Leaving all his equipment bar his dressing bag, he set off down the road with his load. Shells began to explode on the road making the job even harder as he had to leave the road and carry on over rough ground. At last a motor ambulance was found and the patient was handed over:

> "He emptied his pockets seeking something to express his gratitude but
> I needed none such. The sheer look of thankfulness on his face was all
> I needed."

Once more he set off in search of "D" Company. Coming across a dump
of abandoned equipment he was able to aquire a new set of kit but no stretcher,
and "D" Company was eventually located in front of the wood and the village
of Adinfer. It was now late evening and Pearson found himself a hole to settle
down in to rest, ignoring the spasmodic rifle and machine-gun fire. The next
morning saw much activity on his right where the Guards were holding the
line:

> "Jerry resumed his attack early-doors on our right, where the Guards
> Brigade were now in position, but he was not able to move them."

On March 31st, Pearson's unit was relieved by the 15th Highland Light
Infantry and after a night's rest in billets they were taken by bus back to
Monchy Breton:

> "How lovely it was to be able to have a shave once more followed by
> a bath however primitive the conditions."

Fresh clothing was issued to the men, boosting their morale. Pearson knew
the line had held, even though they had been forced back, and he looked
with hope to the future. He was not one of the outstanding participants in
the March retreat but he had been involved in all the horrors and dangers
suffered by units taking part. As a stretcher-bearer he had exposed himself
to great personal danger and speaks in his diary of performing acts of great
courage as part of the everyday work required of a stretcher-bearer. The front-
line troops admired the coolness shown by stretcher-bearers who showed
scant regard for their own safety but would risk life and limb to save others.
These men were treated with great respect as every soldier in the line knew
the next man who needed rescuing could be himself.

After the March offensive had been halted, the German Army that had overrun British areas were dismayed to find the enemy stores well stocked with
all kinds of equipment; it was obvious that the British forces were better
equipped than they were and demoralization began to set in. [6]

On April 9th, the second German offensive opened in Flanders towards
Hazebrouck and created a hole thirty miles wide and five miles deep.
Passchendaele was abandoned, which had been won at a terrible cost in lives
the previous year, and Haig feared the Channel ports would be captured. His
famous order of the day was issued on April 12th:

> "With our backs to the wall and believing in the justice of our cause each
> one of us must fight to the end."

Four French divisions were thrown into the fighting and on 29th April the

German advance once more ground to a halt. The retreat by the British forces was not all orderly and in parts of the line it was considered by some to be a complete rout. Lt. Slack of the 1/4th East Yorkshires said that it was the only time that he thought the war lost. [7]

The Guards were in the Arras sector during the March attacks and Capt. E. D. Ridley records in his diary:

"Pretty windy, I thought the wind pretty bad at Arras." [8]

Osborne's record of part of a Guards unit breaking bears this out. When the March assault came, troops in the very front were overwhelmed by vastly superior numbers and not only the Guards broke:

"It was about this time that men were running away with staring eyes and having discarded their rifles; one could do nothing to stop them." [9]

Every battle has some point when fear sweeps through the troops, but unless it leads to a complete rout no particular unit would be singled out for punishment. This collapse of morale was not common among British troops and if any proof is required that the vast majority of men stood their ground offering devoted resistance, one needs only to look at the German casualties for March and April, 1918.

During the German assaults of March and April, the 11th East Yorkshires had 144 other ranks killed and the whole Battalion was reduced to the strength of a Company. The 10th East Yorkshires had 145 other ranks killed and both units suffered many more wounded or taken prisoner. [10]

By the end of the March/April offensives the British Army had met one hundred and nine enemy Divisions and fought them to a standstill. No strategic gains had been won by the Germans and they had suffered 250,000 casualties. They had captured 1,200 square miles of territory and inflicted 80,000 casualties on the French and 160,000 casualties on the British. 90,000 British troops were taken prisoner in the first days of the battle.

For our final part of this section we will now follow the fortunes of Peter McNally who joined the 2nd Hull Pals in 1914 and served with them until early 1918 when he was transferred to the 1/4th East Yorkshires. The diary he has left covers the period from May 26th to October 5th, 1918, and in it he describes his part in resisting the German offensive of May and life as a prisoner of war. He wrote his diary in Giessen prisoner of war camp, Lazarette Hospital, Germany.

The 1/4th East Yorkshires had been all but wiped out in the German offensive on the Somme and after receiving new drafts of men had been deployed on a quiet part of the line. They were sent to the sixth French Army on the Aisne but did not know at the time that this was where the next hammer-blow was to fall. The French in this sector captured a prisoner who told them of the coming attack. [11] Company Sgt. Maj. McNally (later Regimental Sgt. Maj.) begins his diary in the support line on the 26th May, the day before the expected offensive.

Up to the 26th May it had been a quiet time for 1/4th East Yorkshires and they had been expecting to be relieved at any time:

> "I heard that Fritz was going to strafe us."

Later on the 26th "B" Company joined McNally's "C" Company and his comment on the former was:

> "Had the wind up properly."

While he was doing the rounds at 1 a.m. a fierce bombardment came down upon the British line:

> "It was awful, about the worst I had ever known. I had only just time
> to get a bit of cover when shells burst all around."

After a while the barrage eased and McNally found his Captain and they both went to check on the men. They had all put on their gas masks as the smoke was thick; McNally forgot to do this and got a taste of the fumes. No men had been killed yet but the barrage continued.

Cpl. Peter McNally, 11th East Yorks

No contact could be made with other parts of the front or rear areas as all wires had been cut and runners could not get through. Those that had been sent out never returned. It was not until 5 a.m. that a runner arrived from Battalion Head Quarters with orders to deploy along a certain trench. McNally hurried his men into position, as it was thought the enemy were now advancing, and called up all the men from dug-outs telling them to bring their guns and ammunition with them:

"Our position was not a good one, we were just below the hill. We soon

> rallied our men. I spotted some Germans about fifteen yards away coming
> along the communication trench. They spotted us too and wanted us to
> surrender. I fired my revolver at them and they turned back. More of them
> were coming in on our left and I saw one coming over the hill. I told one
> of my men to pot him, he sent him down for the count. Soon we were
> hard at it with little chance for the enemy was above and all around us."

McNally took cover in a shell hole and bullets were striking the ground only
inches away from him. He tried to spot the gunner but it was impossible:

> "I meant to try to get him if I had."

He and his men were forced to retire and found themselves on a small hill
totally surrounded. The battle raged about them and it was obvious the enemy
was master of the field. All links with other units had been lost and it was
now a case of every man for himself. McNally made a dash for it in the direction of the enemy and dived and crawled from shellhole to shellhole:

> "I saw Sgt. Scott get into a shellhole. I joined him. He had been got in
> the body. I did all I could for him, I stayed with him until he begged of
> me to go. I told him to pray and went at last."

As he left Sgt. Scott his helmet was struck. Taking it off he found a hole
in it as big as a penny through both sides; luckily he escaped injury. McNally
prayed as he stumbled on, feeling utterly worn out, until he reached a road
where dead bodies were strewn across the ground. Still he carried on, meeting
one of his friends, Eddie Kilkenny, but soon lost him again in the confusion.
At last he came to a dugout occupied by a Frenchman and some wounded
Englishmen; he stayed for a drink and a rest and was told they were about
four kilometres from Magie. German planes flew overhead but no sign was
to be seen of any British airmen. More French troops joined the group and
they all decided to make a dash for it even though the road was under heavy
fire. As they rushed out German machine-guns opened up on them, immediately felling many of the Frenchmen:

> "It was really miraculous that I missed being hit, some of the French fell
> hit badly. I took cover in some long grass. It would be as nearly as I could
> guess about 10 a.m. There was a small group of men near the wood, I
> joined them and found my pal Fred Oliver was one of them. We shook
> hands and said what a pleasant meeting it was."

The group did their best to get away but found the enemy all around them.
As darkness fell the men were feeling very cold and hungry and had been
reduced to drinking water from a shell-hole. An empty dug-out was found
and the group decided to spend the night there and surrender the next
morning.

At 7 a.m. the next day McNally and his comrades left their dug-out to find
a glorious summer's day. They came across another group who were being

escorted by German soldiers and joined them. So the fighting ended for Company Sgt. Maj. McNally. He had done his duty and stuck to his post until forced out by a numerically superior attacking force. Even when it was obvious all was lost, he and his pals tried to find a way back to their own lines until no hope of escape was left. His diary shows no trace of bitterness or disillusion and like his comrades he carried on his part of the war to the last. The next part of his diary describes the experience of the prisoner-of-war.

McNally sold his watch for ten francs as he guessed he would lose it anyway and the band of prisoners were marched to Ramicourt in hot oppressive weather. Wounded men were carried in greatcoats as no stretchers were available. The roads were thick with dust and lined with dead whose boots had been removed. As he marched, McNally met an officer of the Royal Garrison Artillery (Hull) and gave him 50 francs to look after for him:

> "I believe he is called Hartley and is a padre. He lives on the Anlaby Road in Hull."

Ramicourt was reached about 6 p.m. The place was in ruins and hundreds of French and British prisoners were milling around. McNally bartered his puttees for a bit of sour black bread:

> "The men gave almost anything for bread — watches, rings and even £1 notes for a little loaf. I got a thick slice for 3 francs and ten English cigarettes and counted myself very lucky. The particular Gerry I bartered with happened to want a smoke for some of the men offered far greater value."

This was to be McNally's first food for two days. Food, its acquisition and quality was to be a permanent problem in the next few weeks. The condition of the men gradually disintegrated as each man was expected to work for his meagre share of sustenance. His first night in captivity was to be spent in a filthy, stinking building at Ramicourt, but as the prisoners filed in there was no room for McNally and he spent the night under a hedge in the cold; he had no coat or blankets and spent a miserable night:

> "What I saw of the German transport was a surprise to me, they used any sort of old carts and horses and even donkeys."

The German troops were not well supplied with equipment and as has been stated earlier were dismayed to find captured British stores well stocked with everything.

The only way to escape the misery of the prison camp was to go on working parties to do all manner of manual work. The men were unshaven, unwashed and covered from head to toe with dust. All the men were lousy and getting weaker by the day. It was all they could do to march home at night after a hard day.

In the morning German guards with big sticks would rouse the men and any that did not move immediately were badly beaten by their captors:

> "It made one wild to see such brutality. Our men were so weak and had

had neither wash nor shave."

Thoughts of home occupied the men constantly and they wondered when they would be able to let their families know they were still alive. As far as the people at home were concerned they would simply be listed as missing in action.

On June 4th McNally went out with a working party in glorious weather to bury the British dead. The badly decomposed bodies were unrecognizable as they had inflated and blackened in the hot weather. On some were found paybooks with names inside and the information contained was written on makeshift crosses that were hurriedly put together. The German troops had stripped the dead of their boots, puttees, trousers and anything in their pockets:

"They looked awful and smelt worse. In three days we buried about fifty including Capt. Hinglebury, our Adjutant. Large numbers of Yorks. we had not time to bury. There was a dead Boche with a whole loaf at his side, we did not scruple to eat the loaf. Buried Pte. Carlisle, 15 Louvaine Road, Preston."

Theft in the prison camp was rife. Nothing could be left around and hunger drove men to steal rations from their own mates, a thing they would never have dreamed of doing in the front line.

On June 17th, McNally and a party of men were marched away from the squalor of the camp to an unknown destination. At various points they were handed over to other escorts, some of which were not always friendly. At 7.30 a.m. on the 18th, cavalry took over as escort and did all they could to make life wretched for the British:

"They were the worst we ever had dealings with. If we sang they ran us down, if we smiled or spoke they made their horses knock into us. Our destination, our escort told us, was twenty kilos away, they liked telling us unhappy things."

Food was given to the Tommies at resting points but the march was the worst McNally had experienced. At their current location on the 19th there was little to do between meals and the men slept during these long hours of boredom:

"We have little pride left now, seeing some men boiling potato peelings in a tin hat we got some too and a few whole spuds and a bucket."

McNally ended his journey to Germany by train. At Giessen prison camp he found conditions much improved and the food also. McNally's unselfish assistance in aiding wounded soldiers in the Lazarette Hospital was a talking-point among the men and many in the camp who would not have survived had it not been for his help willingly shared their rations with him. After the war a letter was published in The Hull Daily Mail from Sgt. P. V. Kay, 1st East Yorkshires praising him:

"I should like to thank the late Company Sgt. Maj. McNally of "C"

Company, 1/4th East Yorkshires, for his great kindness and assistance to sick and wounded prisoners of war. . . . . At a great risk to his own health, this large hearted man came daily into that den of disease and filth to render whatever aid he could to his comrades.'' [12]

Giessen Prisoner-of-War camp. Soldiers of different nationalities were kept here. C.S.M. McNally was interned here until the end of the war.

McNally's war was over. It was now October, 1918; he thought now of his immediate comrades and of his loved ones at home. Hope could again find a place in him as rumours began to fly of the advance of the Allies. In a month the Armistice would be signed and he and his pals would be returning home to normality and home life.

The last German offensive came on July 15th, and was soon halted by the French. On July 18th the French counter-attacked the German flank aided by tanks and pushed them back four miles. So the tide of war turned at the Marne, just where it had turned in 1914. This signalled the start of a general Allied offensive.

Ludendorf had pinned his hopes on complete victory and anything less left the German forces in a desperate situation. Because of the casualties suffered in the advance the temporary advantage of fresh troops from the Eastern Front was soon gone. The crack troops that had led the offensives were irreplaceable and could only be substituted by inferior drafts. By the middle of 1918 the Allied resources were far superior to the Germans' and the losses suffered since March were now being replaced by the influx of American troops. The many complex reasons for the German capitulation lie beyond the bounds of this study, but the end of the Great War was not just a German capitulation, it was a great victory for the Allied Armies. They faced a still powerful and unbroken army and imposed their will on it. Britain played a large part in this and drove a great segment of the German army from one position to another. By November, 1918, it was evident that if this continued it would end in a total allied victory. The only choices left to the German forces were to capitulate while still on conquered territory or be forced back fighting into the Fatherland and be compelled to abandon the contest there.

NOTES

1. Hilyard, H. Pte. 37901, Hull Commercials. Killed in action, 12th April, 1918. Formerly 5/41280, Northumberland Fusiliers. (Documents in Author's collection).
2. Spencer S. L/Cpl. 200661, 1/4th East Yorkshires. 6th January, 1918, Letter home. Hull Local History Library. (Died of gangrene shortly after Armistice).
3. Ibid.
4. History of the 10th (Service) Battalion, East Yorkshire Regiment. (Brown and Sons, Hull, 1924) p.138.
5. The History of the 10th spells it as Hamelincourt.
6. Taylor, A. J. P. The First World War (Penguin, 1987) p.221.
7. Slack, C. Lt. Taped interview (1980). Author's collection.
8. Wilson, T. Myriad Faces of War. (Polity Press, 1986) p.552.
9. Slack, C. M. Grandfather's Adventures in the Great War. (Stockwell Ltd., 1977) p.214.
10. Soliders died in the Great War. Part 20, The East Yorkshire Regiment. (Heywood and Son, 1989) pp.57-75.
11. Wyrral, E. The East Yorkshire Regiment in the Great War. (Harrison and Sons, 1928) p.317.
12. Letter from P. V. Kay, July 8th, 1919. (Author's collection).

CHAPTER ELEVEN

'Not a Mere Collection of Men'

A T DAWN on the 8th August, 1918, 2,000 British guns opened up a terrific bombardment on the enemy lines. 400 tanks, followed by waves of infantry, crossed no-man's-land at 4.20 a.m., completely crushing the German defences and capturing 13,000 prisoners. By nightfall on that day the British troops had advanced nearly seven miles into enemy territory between Albert and Villiers Bretonneux. This day was described by Ludendorff as the "Black day of the German Army", [1] and it was certainly the beginning of the end for Germany.

The 10th and 11th East Yorkshires had had time to refill their dwindling ranks in the period before the British attack and received many new drafts from England. New tactics were now in operation and a process of nibbling away at the German defences was undertaken. Major strongpoints were often by-passed and left to the follow-up troops to deal with. The men advanced in small parties and not in extended lines as they did on the Somme and at Oppy.

During the advance the Hull Units were constantly in and out of the line, and it was not to be an easy affair as the enemy often put up a stout defence and gave ground only when killed, taken prisoner or forced back. On the night of 12th September alone the 11th Battalion had six officers wounded, one missing, twenty-five other ranks killed, seventy-one wounded and forty-four missing. [2]

When a town or village was entered the civilians hailed the East Yorkshiremen as heroes and cheered them through the street. Ploegsteert Wood (Plugstreet Wood) was passed and the River Lys crossed:

> "Now beginning to enter territory hitherto held all the war by the Germans and great was the joy of the villagers we now met. . . . . Great was the jubilation as we entered Roubaix, an experience which none will forget I'm sure." [3]

In Roubaix flags fluttered from the buildings and flowers and bottles of wine were thrust upon the conquering heroes. Pandemonium ensued and all order was lost, an experience repeated in each suburb of the town they passed through. The men were meant to be billeted in farm buildings but the townspeople would have none of it and took the astounded Tommies into their own homes:

> "My pal and I found ourselves in a lovely home among working class people who could not do enough for us." [4]

Food and drink was provided and Pearson and his pal were even given the use of a feather bed but found it hard to sleep at first in such comfort. The luxuries were much appreciated but Pearson and his pal were concerned that these good people were going without themselves. After nearly a week the party ended and the troops moved on to pursue the now retreating enemy.

German troops retreat before the victorious British forces, 1918

Booty was to be found in plenty during the advance as German troops had helped themselves to the contents of shops and left them scattered about the streets. The Tommies, however, were reluctant to pick things up as booby-traps had been left for unsuspecting British troops:

> "I spotted a piano and longed to sit down and have a tune but was reminded of the booby-trap and refrained." [3]

The 10th and 11th East Yorkshires crossed the River Escaut and landed on its eastern side on 9th November. Resistance was still being met at this stage but it was not serious and soon overcome, enabling the units to push on.

In billets on the night of the 9th rumours began to circulate that the war was over; the men however had heard it all before and settled down to rest after a hard day. Outside, artillery fire and the whine of shells could still be heard and stretcher-bearers were bringing in wounded to the regimental aid post.

On the 10th November, Pearson was marching with the Hull Commercials along a road packed with advancing troops. He noticed a car weaving its way through the traffic and flying above it was a big white flag. He pointed this out to his mate, then it was gone from sight and out of Pearson's thoughts. Pte. Ernest Land in the transport section of the 11th Battalion also spotted the car but did not realize its significance. The men inside were important German officials and high-ranking officers, sent to negotiate an armistice with the now victorious Allies.

The night of 10th November saw the 11th Battalion on the high ground round Flobecq forming an outpost line. The 10th Battalion was at Haisette in billets just west of Flobecq.

Pte. Pearson of the 10th Battalion settled down for the night with his pals in a badly battered convent and had to sleep on cold tiles. During the early hours of 11th November he could stand the cold no longer, so he put his boots on and stepped outside for a smoke. As he sat there alone in the dark enjoying his cigarette a runner came by and told him of the Armistice, to become effective at 11 a.m.:

> "And so it had really come (The Armistice). The moment to which we had been looking forward for four long years had really come, no more parades, inspections or going over the top. Now that it had come we just couldn't believe it or what to do with it, there was no enthusiasm whatsoever. For myself a time of bewilderment." [3]

At the time the Armistice was reported in the early hours of 11th November a fierce bombardment was in progress on the left of the 'Hull Pals' making some of them doubt the validity of this report. [4] During the morning the barrage subsided until that momentous hour was reached, 11 a.m., and the guns fell silent.

Pte. Pearson recalled that hour many years later:

> "I'm ashamed to say that I cannot remember if I even paused a moment to offer up prayer of thanksgiving to God for my safe deliverance. I can only remember withdrawing from the little group I was with and retiring to a corner of what had once been the convent garden. Just to be alone, perhaps that was my act of thanksgiving." [5]

Men at the front felt a great loss of purpose with the signing of the Armistice. They could now stand up without fear of instant death, no more need they fear the barrage or gas attacks, raids and future battles were no more. Although the civilians went mad celebrating, the fighting men felt confused now it was all over. In the words of L/Cpl. Beeken of the Hull Commercials:

> "The war was over, what an anti-climax!" [6]

Men who enlisted in the Commercials (10th East Yorks) in 1914, photographed at St Omer in 1919.

Men who enlisted in the 11th East Yorks in 1914, photographed at St Omer in 1919.

Bandsman Lewis Stephenson Osborne, of the 11th Battalion, who had been badly wounded in the March offensives was on the mend by November, 1918, and was graded BIII. He was travelling by train to Hull on 11th November when the train pulled into York Station where there was great excitment. The Armistice had been signed. Girls from the local Rowntree's factory filled the Station and decked the locomotive in red, white and blue:

"On arrival at Hull, great excitement, everyone goes mad, all work ceases, fireworks, etc. Stan and I walk through town, feelings indescribable." [7]

Elsie Swift remembers vividly the street parties in Hull to celebrate the end of the war. She was twelve years old then and lived in Bean Street. Flags and bunting decorated the street and her grandmother, who was very old in 1918, sat in a wicker chair: spread out before her on a table was a table-cloth she had made which featured the flags of all the allies.

The 10th and 11th East Yorkshires were ordered back to France with the Fifth Army and slowly began to wend their way back over familiar ground. In late November both units found their final resting place in St. Omer where they were billeted to await further orders. On Christmas Day, 1918, both units enjoyed a veritable feast served by their own N.C.O.'s:

"Plenty of turkey and plum pudding flavoured with rum, with free beer for those who wanted it. A good time was seemingly had by all." [8]

After Christmas men were being sent home on demobilization leave in preparation for the total disbandment of the Hull units. Many soldiers were not satisfied with the speed of demobilization and disturbances broke out in Calais. The Hull Commercials were ordered to Calais at once to quell any disorder:

"Imagine our amazement when at 4 a.m. (29th January) we were all awakened by the orderly sergeant and ordered to an early breakfast and to be on parade, battle order, by six o'clock." [8]

At Calais the whole of the 31st and 35th Divisions were assembled. Men of the Royal Army Ordnace Corps had seized store-houses. Representatives of the mutineers met General Sir W. R. Birchwood who listened to their demands and by 1 p.m. on the 30th January it was all over. The Battalion was ordered back to St. Omer the same day. Armourer-Sgt. Good, late of the Battalion Signal Section and of "D" Company, lost his life in the riots at Calais. The details of this upheaval do not concern this study as the Hull units were only briefly involved. An excellent account of the events leading up to the intervention by British troops can be found in Andrew Rothstein's The Soldiers' Strikes of 1919.

Men continued to be sent home a few at a time until only a cadre was left. This small force, consisting of 4 officers and 37 men of the Commercials and 3 officers and 35 men of the 11th Battalion, left France and arrived at Southampton on Thursday, 22nd May, 1919. From here they were sent into

Men of the Commercials load a German mobile cooker, captured late in the war, on to transport for home. This trophy was paraded through the city in May 1919.

Troops march past Hull City Hall

billets at Sheffield on Friday night and arrived in Hull, along with the cadre of the 145th Heavy Battery (formerly 3rd Hull Heavy Battery) [9] on the morning of Monday, 26th May. The Hull Daily Mail announced on the 27th:

"HULL WELCOMES ITS WARRIORS". [10]

Between 10.30 a.m. and 11 a.m. the Hull Pals arrived at Paragon Station where a gathering of military and civic dignitaries, headed by the Lord Mayor (Councillor P. Gaskell) and Lord Nunburnholme, welcomed the returning troops. Outside the station a great crowd had assembled to see the homecoming and every point of vantage was occupied. Children lined the railings; windows, balconies and rooftops were packed with spectators on that bright sunny day when hardly a breeze unfurled the limply hanging flags. Cheers rang out from inside the station as the troops marched out and formed up in the square where the Cenotaph now stands.

A particular feature of the Commercials was a captured German field cooker that had been taken at Vitroy towards the end of the war. It was to accompany them in the parade. Demobilized men formed up at the rear of the cadres, the bands got their instruments ready and the Battalion's colours, displaying all their hard-won battle honours, were unfurled. Not all the men who survived were able to take part in the march. Ex-Pte. Cottrell of the 11th Battalion attended the proceedings in a hand-propelled carriage — he had lost both his legs at Arras.'' [11]

The assembled ranks were inspected and then addressed by Lord Nunburnholme:

> "A hearty welcome and also a greeting to your old comrades out of khaki. In the name of the King I thank you for the splendid service you have rendered the Country." [12]

Once the formalities were over orders were barked out and the troops marched off, reaching the Monument Bridge at 12.30 p.m. Hundreds of people lined the route from the bridge to the Guildhall and as the troops marched proudly to the regimental march, 'The Yorkshire Lass', the crowd gave them a rapturous welcome, waving flags, cheering and singing the National Anthem:

> "The haunting strains of the band playing fell pleasantly upon the ears of the 92nd Brigade — relatives and citizens had been waiting eagerly and patiently for these joyous moments — There were, alas, others for whom the day held only memories." [12]

At the middle door of the Law Courts on Alfred Gelder Street the Lord Mayor and a large party took the salute as the troops marched past, proceeding to the square at the Lowgate end of the Guildhall in front of the statue of Lord Nunburnholme. Here they were addressed by the Lord Mayor from the balcony as the crowds filled the whole area:

> "We welcome you home to your wives and families and your friends. Our deliverance is due to you, for your heroic conduct amidst great danger.

The cadre of the 10th East Yorks, Hull Commercials, at Hull Paragon station, 26th May, 1919.

The cadre of the 11th East Yorks at Paragon station, 26th May, 1919.

> You have offered to lay down your lives for our Country's service and
> the sacrifices made are held in honour. We regret there are many who
> will not return and our sympathies go out to those who have to mourn
> their loss.'' [12]

The Mayor talked of the upheavals industry had gone through and of how
employers and employed should pull together in order to allow trade to return
to normal. Work for all demobilized men should be available after they had
had a well-earned rest. A plea was made to employers to do all in their power
to find work for ex-soldiers. The Mayor finished by inviting the men to light
refreshments in the banqueting room and the officers to luncheon. Before
being dismissed the soldiers were asked to look at a photograph on display
in the Guildall of Pte. W. Loftus of the North Yorkshire Regiment. He was
reported missing and it was hoped the homecoming troops might have some
news of him, but none did.

So ended the story of the Hull Pals, a story of ordinary people caught up
in momentos events. The new armies of the Pals Divisions were proud to
be called Kitchener's men. They possessed an esprit de corps that was due
to their most important characteristic, their social cohesion. Their powerful
sense of local identity sprang mainly from the way in which they were raised.
Officers knew their men intimately and often personally, units trained together
and stayed together in the field. This produced a sympathy and awareness
between all ranks in the new armies that was of great value on active service.
The men of the Hull Pals never forgot this and the personal bonds formed
in the trenches were to last a lifetime.

Pte. Pearson attended the final parade in civilian clothes and was glad to
be back with his pals once more. Of the Commercials he commented:

> ''These men were volunteers, not conscripts or national service men, and
> as such fought as a family unit from the beginning and not as a mere collec-
> tion of men.'' [13]

The final act in the history of Hull's Service Battalions was to be the laying
up of the colours in Holy Trinity Church in the city centre. They are still there
to this day, displaying all of the hard-won battle honours paid for in blood
and pain, and all who search for their story can still find scattered around
the city other memorials. Street rolls of honour still exist in Dansom Lane,
Sharp Street, Marfleet Avenue and Eton Street. Dozens of these memorials have
disappeared over the years as the city forgets the sacrifice these young men
made and their story slips quietly from living memory and into the realms
of history.

Reginald Pearson pondered in his diary as to the lack of recognition given
to these forgotten warriors:

> ''But I never forget them even though the nation may and I wonder is
> the nation worthy of them and their sacrifice?'' [13]

NOTES

1. Wyrall, E. The East Yorkshire Regiment in the Great War. (Harrison and Sons Ltd., 1928). p.333.
2. War Diary. 11th East Yorkshires, 12th September, 1918. (Prince of Wales Own Museum, York).
3. Pearson, R. Pte. 10/1180, Hull Commercials, 1915-1918. Diary. (Author's collection).
4. By some of them. A short diary of the 11th (S) Battalion, East Yorkshire Regiment. (Browns, Hull, 1921) p.69.
5. Pearson, R. Diary.
6. Beeken, J. L/Cpl. 10/685, Hull Commercials, 1916-1918. Diary. (Author's collection).
7. Osborne, L. S. Pte. 11/341, 11th East Yorkshires, 1914-1918. Diary. (Author's collection).
8. Pearson, R. Diary.
9. 3rd Hull Heavy Battery, raised in Hull in October, 1915. Sent to France in June, 1916.
10. Hull Daily Mail. 27th May, 1919.
11. Pte. Cottrell, 11th East Yorkshires. Lived in Hull at 3 Cobden Place, Norfolk Street, Beverley Road.
12. Hull Daily Mail. 27th May, 1919.
13. Pearson, R. Diary.

CHAPTER TWELVE

Trials and Tribulations

KILLING

T HE OFFICIAL ATTITUDE to the enemy was straighforward. All front-line troops were expected to be implacably hostile to the Germans and kill them whenever the opportunity arose. Propaganda in the Hull newspapers published reports of German outrages and atrocities against civilians in order to foster this ruthless spirit, and the large majority of people believed what they were told, at least in the first two years of the war.

The Hull Service Battalions were not regular troops and before their service in France had no opportunity to fire their rifles in anger. The young men from Hull had yet to take a life and some put off that moment until they were left with no choice but to kill another human being:

> "I caught glimpses of inquisitive Germans popping their heads over the parapet. However I did not open fire on them, for I do not intend to stain my hands with blood until the necessity arrives." [1]

wrote Pte. Graystone 1916.

Others relished their work and would take every opportunity to do their duty as a soldier and bag any German who presented himself as a target. Cecil Slack of 1/4th East Yorkshires wrote in 1916:

> "I had a couple of shots at what I thought was a German, I don't know whether I killed anything but I tried hard." [2]

Men would kill without emotion when revenge was the motive. Lt. Slack wrote home of his feelings when killing Germans and confessed his emotions were quite normal even when he had to walk over the man's dead body to carry on his work. "We remember the air raids (on Hull) on that occasion" he said. [3] The loss of friends would provoke usually sedate men into acts of fearful violence. One night in 1916 Pte. Horsfield of the Hull Commercials was blown to pieces by a shell in a communication trench; his mates took their revenge and spent the night killing whole German working parties that were usually allowed to do their work. The killing of enemy troops in such a situation would be done in cold blood without any feeling:

"The lads aren't half avenging his death. The machine guns have been rattling all night, bombs are being thrown and our snipers are very busy." [4]

Whether a man killed in anger, as an act of revenge, or simply because it was has duty, many of them carried a great guilt with them after the war. Pte. Weasenham would express great sorrow when reflecting upon his days in the killing zone and remembers the pity he felt as he killed and maimed. When on trench raids men would be in a maximum danger situation; quarter would seldom be given unless prisoners were required for interrogation and when in doubt about their own safety men would kill even unarmed Germans. On June 26th, 1916, Lt. Slack found himself in the enemy front line in an uncertain situation with only one frightened Tommy and two wounded Germans. The Germans were promptly killed and in Slack's memoirs one can sense a hint of guilt even as the act was committed:

"I slit his neck to the backbone and thought of his parents. I heard his gurgle and felt the froth of his warm blood on my hands." [5]

Even when men could not see the Germans they killed, some found it a most disturbing experience and never fully came to terms with the act of taking life. Pte. Sammy Cook of the Commercials was keen to take part in a trench raid on 18th September, 1916. After the raid it was being discussed by a group of the men behind the lines and Pte. Beeken writes in his diary of that year how surprised he was at Cook's remarks:

"I heard voices coming from a shelter so I lobbed in a grenade. There was an explosion and I heard cries of pain, I thought it is some poor mother's son." [6]

Cook was very shaken at this experience and it disturbed him for a long time afterwards. Despite the reservations of individual consciences, all front-line troops killed in situations of danger; the memoirs left by Hull men all speak of their fear and dislike of this mostly unseen enemy who would have projected into them all the many fears and resentments of soldiers under high stress. An enemy who had killed so many of one's friends and who would shoot Tommies without a conscience had to be loathed.

THE ENEMY

Hatred of enemy troops did not mean they were not admired for their professionalism and for occasional acts of kindness. Pte. Graystone spoke with praise about German troops regarding an indident on the Somme in 1916. A wounded man was lying in no-man's-land in great pain and, despite orders to the contrary, three of his mates went out to fetch him. No shots were fired as he was brought in and once in the safety of the front line it was discovered that his wounds had been dressed by the German troops. Pte. Graystone wrote in his diary:

"Our estimate of the enemy has gone up considerably in consequence." [7]

All front-line troops resented any libels on the courage of German soldiers and would react angrily when such opinions were voiced by non-combatants. Many years after the war, in 1965, Pte. Weasenham was at a family gathering at 17/16th Avenue, North Hull Estate, when a rather foolish young man began to slander German soldiers. Robert Weasenham, a usually easy-going man, turned on him with feeling and put him in his place. Even after such a long time and after experiencing another World War, his attitude to German troops had not changed and was just as strong. [8]

Family gathering, Summer 1965. Robert Harris and Olive Bertha Weasenham (centre) celebrate their Golden Wedding at 17/16th Avenue, North Hull Estate. The photograph on the back wall is of Robert in uniform in 1914. (The author is third from the right).

This kind of respect, even when grudgingly given, was constant and could at times even develop into warmer feelings as in the famous Christmas truces of 1914. Even today it seems odd that men who hated an enemy could come to terms with him on certain days, yet the next day recommence the killing as though nothing had happened. Danger, at whatever level, seems to have been the answer. As it subsided so too did the level of aggression that a soldier was keyed up to respond to. Even in the most active sectors this slackening of aggression would occur for short periods, but as long as the offensive spirit existed the war could be kept up. As any immediate sense of danger subsided men still had to remain alert and distrustful of the enemy.

The different kinds of German regiments opposite the Hull Pals when in the line were well known, but the two that stand out in the memories of the men were the Prussians and the Saxons. The Prussians were known as fierce and constant fighters. Pte. Barker and Pte. Weasenham both said that when they were faced with Prussian troops they would have a hard time of it as they were constantly raiding, sniping and bombing. The Saxons on the other hand were less martial and liked an easier time. One night in 1916 Pte. Weasenham remembers them calling to him when on sentry duty:

"We are Saxons, you are Anglo-Saxons, come over to us tommy." [9]

The men laughed and shouted back; the Saxons threw over sausage and the Tommies threw back tins of beef.

A brave, tenacious and at times merciful enemy was respected by all experienced front-line troops. They appreciated that German men had found themselves in the same predicament as the Tommies and each side could feel the bond of shared tribulation. When asked how he felt about German troops, Albert Barker replied:

"I didn't hate them, they were the same as us, we all did our duty." [10]

Though respect was felt there was no love or liking; when in a hostile environment Tommies would shoot any Germans they came across, and if the situation was doubtful in some way they would kill them to save themselves. The will to survive was rarely absent from troops in the line and their obedience to duty kept them going in the most terrible conditions.

OFFICERS

The way men thought of their leaders varied from individual to individual. Officers would be obeyed without question throughout the War and this ranged from the heady days of 1914 through the much darker years that followed. There is no record of any insubordination among the 'Hull Pals' and the diaries they left show that as far as the rank and file were concerned there were two distinct types of officer: those that led from the rear and never saw the front line and those that led their men from the front, sharing all hardships and dangers. The latter were naturally regarded with great esteem and affection by the bayonet men.

As the War progressed, men began to notice that those that sent them into offensives were rarely actually seen at the front, and the natural conclusion

The famous 'public relations' photograph of 'D' Coy, 10th East Yorks (Hull Commercials) on the Somme, 3rd July, 1916. (1) Walter Aust (2) C. Hewison (3) G. Tether, killed in action 13th November 1916 (4) J. Hughes (5) E. Hayes (6) Sgt. W. Leech (7) Sgt. 'Nobby' Clark

drawn from this was that the staff in the rear could have no idea of what they sent men into. After the débacle at Serre on 1st July, 1916, Pte. Pearson wondered why no staff officers were to be seen weeks before the 'big push' in or near the forward area. In a rest camp on July 2nd he reflected upon his experience of battle and upon what he had observed in the weeks beforehand:

"Speaking for myself I felt a strange disquiet but kept it to myself." [11]

On 3rd July, Pearson and the rest of the Hull Commercials were enjoying a much-delayed delivery of mail when the order went out: 'Battle order in ten minutes'. The men marched off, loaded up with bombs, extra ammunition, wire cutters, etc., expecting to go back into the line. They soon realized that they were moving away from the line and after some time began to approach their starting point at Bus. It was with this realization that tempers began to break. Orders were sent from the Colonel that the men must put on a cheery smile as a film camera was taking their picture. Thinking the film might get back to Hull, the men obliged. Months later an old newspaper was found and in it was a photograph of the Commercials with the heading: 'Happy East Yorkshires going into action'.

"It is a pity the said newsman cannot hear our comments." [12]

This photograph has been used in various publications and shows happy smiling troops going into action on the Somme, or so it was thought. Pearson registers great displeasure in his diary that the Command should use troops who had just been in action in such a cynical way for a public relations stunt.

When units came out of the line they would often fall foul of officers who insisted on implementing the most petty regulations. In April, 1916, an order was sent to the Hull Commercials complaining that they did not salute a certain General when he drove by them and that in future any man not doing so would suffer field punishment number one for seven days:

"The worst punishment we can have, the wooden solider cad!" [13]

Field punishment number one would involve the victim being lashed to a waggon wheel, spreadeagle style, for a number of hours each day in full view of his comrades.

To make matters worse, others who had lost cap badges, spoons, etc. in the line were put on charges and given doses of C.B. [14] One man was placed on a charge for wrapping the head of his friend, who had been blown to pieces, in his ground sheet: [15]

"This from officers who were in a blue funk when in the trenches, and who never left their dug-outs except when half drunk on the men's rum ration." [16]

At concert parties given in rest areas by the bandsmen, men would take the opportunity to ridicule such offiers, as any man made up in grease-paint

'The Tonics', who entertained the troops in France

and in costume could not be recognised.

> "A man could sing and shout his condemnation of 'Brass Hats' and red-tape with impunity." [17]

These experiences concerning such officers were to be repeated as the war dragged on and left the majority of men with a disbelief in the abilities of the officers running the show, yet the men never broke or questioned orders but maintained a fatalistic acceptance of their role as soldiers.

The young officers who led the men and shared the danger and hardships were not viewed in the same way as these remote beings who sent thousands to their deaths while being miles away themselves. The shared experience of the trenches brought men close together, men that may never have mixed in civilian life and whose life styles at home could be poles apart. In war conditions they found a cameraderie that bridged social barriers and led to insights for them all into the fellowship of feeling experienced by men under such conditions of deprivation and danger.

Pte. Weasenham always spoke with admiration of the young officers that led the men and would never hear a word against them. After the war he remembered all too well how these young men always went over the top first and how many of them were killed in doing so. [18] In the winter of 1916 Co Sgt. Major Carr, 1/4th East Yorkshires, wrote home and mentioned in his letter the officer he served with at the time:

> "The trenches are up to your waist in water and slush and all the time
> you are in there you have to stick it. Your body is shaking with cold and
> you welcome a bullet or a shell to put you out of it altogether.
> God, it is terrible. The one incentive I have is Lt. Slack. He is a thorough
> sport and sticks it. I have shared with him and he with me the sufferings
> of it all." [19]

Kitchener's volunteers found entry into army life difficult and the introduction to trench life even more so. The display of concern shown by some officers made the change tolerable and the hardships bearable; a common purpose bonded officers and men. One desired to be led and the other provided leadership, and if this was tempered by compassion to the lower ranks and a concern for their well-being, a bond was forged that saw them through four years of conflict.

THE DEAD

One unusual aspect of the 'Great War' was the persistent presence of the dead. All the diaries left by members of the 'Hull Pals' speak of the many disturbing sights and unexpected encounters with corpses from both sides. In previous wars battles had lasted only a number of days and had a definite beginning and end; afterwards the dead of both sides would be buried. The 'Great War' was far different and battles could drag on for weeks and months, during which time the front line hardly moved. The entire front was littered with corpses that could not be removed and many that were buried at the front would promptly reappear as the next barrage churned up the ground. In this dark, nightmare world rats grew to enormous size on this vast store of fresh meat, and in the summer months great swarms of black bloated flies would infest

Cpl. Gerald Denis, 21st K.R.R.C.
1915-1919. After the war Gerald
became a teacher and is still living
in Hull.

the trenches and no-man's-land.

This reminder of each man's vulnerability could not be avoided and in every man's mind lurked the thought that every corpse had once been living and breathing like himself. Gerald Denis was in the line for the first time in 1916 when he saw his first man die and recalling the incident still disturbed him 76 years later:

> "I heard no noise at all when my friend collapsed near me. I held him and sat him down next to me and got covered in blood. As I looked into his eyes they began to fade as the life force left him, I couldn't hold him up any longer. This upset me greatly and I felt insecure for many weeks after." [20]

Seeing dead men for the first time was a traumatic experience and few men got used to it, but when corpses had been left for some time in an area of great activity they could make life unbearable for the living. Pte. Graystone, Hull Commercials, had not been in the Somme Valley long when his company was ordered to improve their section of the line by digging it deeper. They soon wished they had left it alone as the stench that came out of the soil was horrible. The dead of previous encounters were found rotting away under-foot and up until now had remained undisturbed:

> "One of the men dug up a little wooden cross supposed to mark the graves of 40 Germans. I hope we do not stumble across their bodies. I have seen one already and it was a ghastly sight." [21]

In such conditions the smell of decomposition permeated everything; even when things were quiet, the constant presence of the dead was brought home to men in most of the things they did. Lt. Slack wrote home complaining about the quality of front line tea in February, 1916:

> "The taste is always the same, dead men. This is horrid, but true." [22]

Men would explore areas of the line not in immediate danger and encounter trenches that had been abandoned full of dead men, men who had often been there for some time. Bandsman Osbourne, 11th East Yorkshires, was on one such foray in the Summer of 1916 when he came across a trench lined with dead West Yorkshires who had been killed on the 1st July: the bodies were badly rat-eaten. Not to be put off he continued his search for souvenirs:

> "Entered Boche dug out — full of dead. Mistook dead German's hair for fur coat, pulled his scalp off." [23]

Others hunting for objects of value would be far more calculating and would go through the pockets of dead men without a second thought. Pte. Weasenham, 11th East Yorkshires, remembered with revulsion how men would cut fingers off corpses to get rings. [24]

Seeing numbers of dead men known only hours before as pals affected even the most hardened soldier. After an attack or after a bombardment men would have to march out of the line past rows of corpses and such a sight was never

A not untypical scene during the Somme campaign in the summer of 1916.

to be forgotten:

> "We were very sad as we filed out of the trenches past the dead lying in Sackville street dump. Very quietly the Battalion marched back to Bus." [25]

The entries in diaries left by Hull men concerning losses are very touching and sincere, and these sights of lost friends would never leave them. Many found it hard to look upon these fearful apparitions. Killing and death had been to these men the ultimate taboo and here they were having to accept it as part of their immediate existence:

> "This afternoon I saw the whole Battalion's dead. The bodies were laid out along the trench side just as they fell. I shall never forget the sight as long as I live. It was hard to look upon them, dear old pals." [26]

The cemeteries behind the lines after an action were kept busy throughout the war as the constant loss of life drained the country of its best young men. Diaries mention touching scenes at burials as men paid their last respects to comrades. As diaries are closed the last remarks speak of lost friends and the happy memories associated with them; there is no bitterness, only a great sadness at the cutting down of young men in their prime. But many men would not have missed their war experience and the great feeling of camaraderie that made men look back on this nightmare with nostalgia.

BACK TO BLIGHTY

To the outsider the levels of endurance to which a front-line soldier was exposed seem beyond belief, but even though men were obedient this does not mean that individuals did not want to escape from the dangers of the front. During the winter of 1916, Lt. Slack wrote home how he did not wish to return to the front and felt no shame about feeling this way. [27] Many men thought like this but felt such a bond with their comrades that a man who was physically able could not get out without losing face in the eyes of his comrades. The only way out with honour for a front line soldier was to get a 'blighty'. This was the term for a wound that was not grievous enough to maim but bad enough to be sent home for a time or even for good. Slack in his memoirs speaks of one man breaking his collar bone in a football match:

"He got no sympathy, he was just told he was a lucky devil." [28]

In the line it was different as a light wound could not be guaranteed; stories in other books abound relating to how men invited wounding. Winter writes of men pumping water with their arms above the trench parapet inviting a sniper's bullet. [29] However, most troops dared not take the risk. Slack echoes nicely the attitudes of the majority of men to receiving a wound:

"I should love to be nicely wounded and yet I don't want to be, you understand the feeling, don't you?" [30]

But men who were hit and who did not expect it were often happy when it was realized it was not too serious. The Hull Commercials were being relieved on 3rd April, 1916, by the Borderers and as the new sentry stepped into a bay to take over, a sniper got him through the shoulder. He fell and began to laugh, and sitting up against the trench side he lit a cigarette. As the stretcher bearers carried him out, envious comments were shouted out at him by his comrades who wished they were in his shoes. [31]

Self-wounding in the army was a serious offence and if a man shot himself the tell-tale powder burns of a close range discharge would be clearly visible. During the retreat of 1918, Pte. Pearson was a witness to such an incident and a very ingenious method was used to eliminate these marks. Pearson came across a farmhouse and heard angry voices. Not sure if they were friend or foe, he looked through a crack and saw two men arguing. It seemed a pact had been made whereby each man would shoot the other through the foot. One had completed his side of the bargain but the other refused to go through with it. A tin of bully beef was placed against the ankle to guard against any marks being left. Pearson only refers to these two men as 'A' and 'B' and does not pass any judgement upon the men's actions. 'A' was seen in Hull after the war by Pearson. [32]

Men would seek a way out of the trenches but few would risk losing face in the eyes of their comrades. It was thought to be bad form to let other men down, but a legitimately-earned wound, or one that could not be proved to be otherwise, was one way out that was yearned for by the majority of soldiers. The longing to see friends and home was overpowering and men would carry with them photographs of loved ones and their letters and keepsakes. Letters and parcels from home were looked forward to with eagerness, and the contact with the old life could lift a man's spirit in the darkest hours and make him realize that the people he loved were still there, supplying the emotional support he needed. Better than this form of contact was home leave, though this tended to be granted in rather an erratic way. Pte. Weasenham never got leave and saw home only after he was wounded at Oppy; Pte. Pearson went two years without leave and then got two within six months.

Being given a pass would cause men to be exultant at the prospect of seeing home; Pte. Graystone sat up in the dead of night, too elated to sleep:

> "No sleep for me last night for I was too excited to think of closing my eyes for a moment." [33]

Sometimes a platoon would receive word that one or two leave passes were available and that if none of the men had already been home, two would have to be chosen. In his diary, Pte. Osborne gives us an insight into how men were picked in such a situation:

> "July 23rd, two men wanted for leave, the fatal card drawing. Ted Stathes drew ace, I drew four, heart drops. Ken Morton drew three, hopes rise. Harry Clarke drew two, still higher hopes." [34]

After this draw for the first leave, the second round began as the three white-faced anxious soldiers, surrounded by the rest of the band, tried their luck. Osborne draws a seven:

> "Ken 4, poor old Nobby 2, tears of excitement." [35]

Without delay the two men packed up their equipment and left the dugout in the early afternoon. Dashing over Vimy Ridge they were in full view of the German lines, but such was their joy that they gave them no thought as they made their first steps towards England.

Though leave was highly prized by the men it was not always an uplifting experience, since they would discover how little civilians knew of the realities of trench life. When Pte. Barker, 13th East Yorkshires, was at home he never even tried to explain to the people there what he had gone through as it was incomprensible to them. [36] Cpl. Denis dare not tell his parents the reality of it all as they would have worried themselves sick. [37] Soldiers about to return to the front would suffer various levels of depression. Paragon Station, Hull, was the scene of many touching goodbyes as young men returned to France, once again leaving the safety and warmth of home life. Men and relatives would realise that this might be the last time they would see each other and so made the parting all the harder.

Legal and illegal means were used to get home by troops. The thought of relief from their sufferings kept them going and, as we have seen, men would take high risks to be back in their own homes. Other men that could stand it no longer would take even greater risks to get out of the war. Nerves could be shattered by shellfire and irreparable damage done to the mind by the sights and pressures of trench warfare and yet men were not recognised to have shell-shock or mental disorders brought on by the conditions they were under. Those that could stand it no longer and ran away risked a death of shame at the hands of their own comrades. These cases were never mentioned by troops that knew of them until many years after the war had ended.

MILITARY EXECUTIONS

The files concerning men shot for leaving their post have never been open to the public. For over seventy years they have been entombed in archives holding a last unknown chapter in the story of the Great War. The general uneasiness felt about this has been proved to be more justified in excellent studies of this subject. I defy anyone to read William Moore's The Thin Yellow Line (1974) and Anthony Babbington's For the Sake of Example (1983) without feeling outrage and horror at the events described. Cases for accused men were rarely presented adequately and sometimes were not presented at all. Capital sentences were passed and sanctioned by senior offices. Mitigating circumstances and the backgrounds of the accused were never properly looked into by the men who made up the court, and in a matter of hours the sentence would be carried out in front of an audience — not voluntary — of the man's own unit.

As we shall see, the effects of an execution on the rank and file were traumatic and men would push it to the backs of their minds, but it was something that was to stay with them for the rest of their lives. The only traceable execution among the ranks of the Hull Pals is of Pte. 11/81 Charles McColl, who enlisted in the Tradesmen's Battalion and was later transferred to 1/4th East Yorkshires. He was a Hull man and lived in the Sculcoates area.

Lt. Slack, 1/4th East Yorkshires, has talked of this event in a taped interview which I possess, but declined to name the man killed:

> "After the Somme offensive we were sent troops who were only remnants of men, not fit, it wasn't their fault they just couldn't stand it. Anyway one man came to us, he wasn't a Hull man, I don't know where he came from, couldn't stand it and ran away. He was brought back and ran away again, this time he was tried and sentenced to death. I had to pick the firing party and put my Sergeant in charge, Len Cavinder. Five of the men had blanks in their rifles and five live rounds and an officer stood by with a loaded revolver to finish the job. The man wasn't fit for military service, he was a half-wit." [38]

200483 Pte. Robert Henry West of Cottingham was on that firing party and was told by the N.C.O. in charge that any man who didn't shoot to kill would find himself in trouble. Pte. West always maintained he shot over his target that day.

Robert Henry West, 1/4th East Yorks, 1914-1919. One of the firing party that executed Charles McColl, Robert West died in Hull in 1973.

Len Cavinder, a Hull man and Sergeant in charge of the firing party, has left us a disturbing account of the execution and the events of the night before it took place. This was published in Dr. A. J. Peacock's excellent magazine 'Gunfire'. [40] At the front near Arras in July, 1917, Cavinder was distributing rations between the men when he noticed the issue seemed over-generous:

> "Now the Quartermaster never sent extra rations up . . . but there were two men left, so they were able to have a cold rabbit each. So there must have been some reason for that, cos' the only reason was that a man was missing."

Nobody had been killed or wounded that night so Sgt. Cavinder reported it

to his superiors. It was not until six months later that Pte. Charles McColl
was found at St. Omer. In December, 1917, Cavinder's Commanding Officer,
Major Jackson, sent him with the Headquarter's Batman, Danby, to Brandhock
to pick up the prisoner and take him to Ypres prison. Cavinder and Danby
were given a Red Cross van for transport and picked up the condemned man:

> "One of the chaps who handed him over to me said, 'He doesn't know
> what's coming to him you know'. I was glad of that."

Ten men had been chosen from Cavinder's platoon to form the firing party.
They had been told what their task was to be, and were kept separate from
their Battalion until it was completed. Each day they practised shooting at
a small piece of white paper, five standing and five kneeling. Every man
received an extra ration of rum.

> "They knew what it was all about but they were sworn to silence, nobody
> had to know."

When asked about the prisoner, Cavinder replied, "He was subnormal
actually. He was unstable. There was something wrong with him . . . I realised
you couldn't get him to slope arms correctly and all that sort of thing. He
wasn't simple but he was slow — but he'd not been too slow to live with
this woman in St. Omer for six months."

Cavinder was to spend a harrowing night with Pte. Charles McColl the night
before the execution and was given half a bottle of whisky and some tablets
with orders to get the prisoner to take them if possible. Danby and Cavinder
tried to avoid the inevitable questions:

> "Why was he being brought to this gaol, what were we going to do with
> him?"

They tried to get McColl to eat and drink but he kept asking questions. Cavinder
put a laudanum tablet in a glass of whisky but the prisoner only drank half
and this had no effect. At midnight a group of red-tabbed officers entered
the cell and read out the death sentence, signed by the King:

> "And if ever I hated King George V . . . but that was it . . . he was like
> a raving maniac for a while."

McColl then settled down but would still not take much whisky; his
photographs were then brought out and he began to hum a popular tune as
he flicked through them. Just then the padre came in and told Cavinder and
Danby to leave while he spoke to him. Cavinder stood at the door and listened
to every word that was said. The Padre told Charles McColl he deserved to
die and that he would be damned if he did not ask for God's forgiveness.
Cavinder, who was a very religious man, could stand to hear no more and
entered the cell:

> "Excuse me sir, I've been asked to help this fellow to find God, but I don't
> think that's the way to do it". The Padre answered, "Alright Sergeant I'll

report you."

Cavinder never saw the Padre again and never wanted to. When things had calmed down he tried to speak to Charles McColl to help him find spiritual peace:

"I wasn't a Parson, but I knew what it was to try to help a chap to lead a better life or ask God's forgiveness — I wanted it myself."

Both men knelt down and said the Lord's Prayer together; although it was mumbled, Cavinder was sure God would understand. The condemned man had to be held down on the bed at times, but just before they came for him he calmed down. At 7 a.m., just as dawn was breaking, two military policemen entered the cell and placed a bag-type respirator [41] on the prisoner's head, with the eye pieces at the back so he could not see. A piece of paper was pinned on his chest. Cavinder shook the man's hand and said "God bless", and his hands were manacled behind him:

"Everybody who took part in it was affected. It was a terrible thing to usher a man into eternity whether it was law or not."

The prisoner was led out into the grey morning light and sat on a chair before a wall. He was strapped in and facing him was the execution squad, five standing, five kneeling. Lt. Riven, standing, revolver in hand, gave the order "fire" and it was all over for Charles McColl:

"I refrain from describing the end, suffice to say the party deputed to bury him were literally shaking with the shock of the ghastly affair."

In fact the stretcher-bearers would not bury the dead man and left the body near the grave for Danby and Cavinder to lay to rest. The body was dropped into the hole already dug. The winter of 1917 was particularly harsh and the ground was frozen solid. The clumps of clay to fill in the grave were frozen and the two men began to drop them on Charles McColl until he was covered. The Padre never turned up so Cavinder, being a devout man, said a few words over the grave.

"No it was a sorry affair altogether .... that was the worst thing that happened to me personally and forever after that, whenever we've gone to Scotland for our holidays .... we've gone to Glasgow and there's a family furnishing firm called by the same name (as the man shot) and it brings it all back."

Lt. Slack wrote home to Charles McColl's family in Hull and told them he had been killed in action and they never had cause to think anything else.

Len Cavinder never revealed the name of the executed man and was haunted by the memory of that frightful event until the day he died. He thought the treatment meted out to McColl far too harsh and noted that in the 1939-45 war he would have received treatment. Indeed, a man of his mental abilities would never have been put in the front line in the Second World War. Pte. Charles McColl's case is featured in Babbington's For the Sake of Example:

though his name is not given, the details provided make it obvious as to the man's identity and give us an insight into the proceedings:

> "He maintained he had been buried by a shell-burst the following September and had been invalided home with heart failure and nerves. When he returned to the Western Front, he said, he shook from head to foot whenever he went into the trenches. Not unnaturally, the court expressed a desire to hear some medical evidence about the man but as none was available did not pursue the matter." [42]

Pte. Charles McColl had no officer to defend him, an unusual feature so late in the war, and was shot on 28th December, 1917. [43]

The discovery of this material came as a great shock to me as I researched the history of the 'Hull Pals', and yet all soldiers knew of this darker side of army life though few would discuss it. To the mass of troops this part of their experience was viewed with disgust and sadness, and soldiers that had to take part in such events felt shame when remembering, though none of them ever refused an order and carried out their duty to 'King and Country'. [44]

NOTES

1. Grayston, J. W. Pte. 10/634, Hull Commercials, 1914-1918. Diary. (Author's collection).
2. Slack, C. M. Grandfather' Adventures in the Great War, 1914-1918. (Stockwell Ltd., 1977) p.34.
3. Ibid.
4. Graystone, J. W. Diary.
5. Slack, C. M. Grandfather's Adventures. p.72.
6. Beeken, J. L/Cpl. 10/685, Hull Commercials, 1914-1918. Diary. (Author's collection).
7. Graystone, J. W. Diary.
8. Weasenham, R. H. Pte. 11/682, 11th East Yorkshires. 1914-1917. (The author attended this gathering).
9. Ibid. Conversation with author, 1960's.
10. Barker, A. Pte. 13th East Yorkshires, 1914-1918. Taped interview, 1988. (Author's collection).
11. Pearson, R. Pte. 10/1180, Hull Commercials, 1915-1918. Diary. (Author's collection).
12. Ibid.
13. Graystone, J. W. Diary.
14. C.B. — Confined to Barracks.
15. Horsefield, Stanley, Pte. Hull Commercials. Lived on Anlaby Common, Hull. Killed by shellfire, 29th March, 1916.
16. Graystone, J. W. Diary.
17. Hull Daily Mail. Peace Edition, 1918. p.16 (Authors collection).
18. Weasenham, R. H. Pte. 11/682, 11th East Yorkshires, 1914-1917. (Conversation with author, 1960's).
19. Slack, C. M. Grandfather's Adventures p.121.
20. Denis, G. Cpl. K.R.R.C. 1915-1918. Taped interview, 1988. (Author's collection).
21. Graystone, J. W. Diary.
22. Slack, C. M. Grandfather's Adventures. p.40.
23. Osborne, L. S. Pte. 11/341, 11th East Yorkshires, 1914-1918. Diary. (Author's collection).
24. Weasenham, R. H. Pte. 11/682, 11th East Yorkshires, 1914-1917. (Conversation with author, 1960's).
25. Beeken, J. Diary.
26. Graystone, J. W. Diary.
27. Slack, C. M. Grandfather's Adventures. p.113.
28. Ibid.
29. Winter, D. Death's Men. (Penguin, 1985) p.228.
30. Slack, C. M. Grandfather's Adventures. p.113.
31. Graystone, J. W. Diary.
32. Pearson, R. Diary.
33. Graystone, J. W. Diary.
34. Osborne, L. S. Diary.
35. Ibid.
36. Barker, A. L/Cpl. 13th East Yorkshires, 1914-1918. Taped interview, 1988. (Author's collection).
37. Denis, G. Cpl. K.R.R.C. 1915-1918. Taped interview, 1988. (Author's collection).
38. Slack, C. M. Lt. 1/4th East Yorkshires, 1914-1918. Taped interview, 1980. (Author's collection).
39. West, R. H. Pte. 200483, 1/4th East Yorkshires, 1914-1918. Conversation with his grandson, Mr. G. Boddy of Cottingham.
40. Peacock, A. J. Gunfire. (York Educational Settlement, Holgate Road, Yorks, 1982) p.3.
41. Gas Mask, Early Type.
42. Babbington, A. For the Sake of Example. (Leo Cooper, 1984) pp.151 and 152.
43. Ibid.
44. Charles Frederick McColl, Pte. 11/81, Born 1891, Sculcoates area, Hull. Shot for desertion 28th December, 1917, aged 26 years. Buried at Ypres Reservoir Cemetery 4/A/6.

Conclusion

O N THE 8th AUGUST, 1914, Lord Kitchener, Secretary of State for War, called for a single increment of 100,000 men to reinforce the regular army. By the Spring of the following year this had increased to 600,000 and five 'New Armies' were formed. In the great industrial cities of the North there was a vast reserve of manpower that made up the Northern contingents of this huge volunteer force. These were the men who formed the "Pals' Battalions".

Of all the countless tales that have their roots in the Great War, perhaps the Pals' story is the most poignant. The recruiting in Hull started slowly during August 1914, until the news of the true situation in Europe could be held back no longer. There arose in September a genuinely spontaneous and popular mass movement the like of which has never been seen before or since.

At the Hull City Hall from September to the start of November, 1914, men joined the service Battalions with their pals and work-mates. The catalysts to mass enlistment were to be the various institutions that gave Edwardian man his sense of identity within a great imperial power like England. Churches, trades unions, rugby clubs, rifle clubs, offices and factories all gave added impetus to British male reactions in the first flush of enthusiasm for the war, and the middle-aged men who appointed themselves raisers of New Armies were not slow to realize this.

The reasons why men enlisted were as diverse as the recruits themselves. Escape from poverty or a boring job and the prospect of excitement all played a part in drawing men forward to take the King's shilling. This is not to say the intense moralistic patriotism of 1914 played a small role in events: the men of Kitchener's New Armies had been brought up at the centre of a great empire that spanned the world and played a major role in international affairs. The attitudes at every level of Edwardian society were formed by the codes of self-sacrifice, discipline and duty.

The declaration of war fused together the elements of nationalistic feeling in Hull into a coherent whole. Once it was realized that the German army was not being stopped and that the fighting was getting ever closer, what had once been a vague shadow in a far-off land become a real enemy that could only be defeated in battle. Men committed themselves willingly to the cause of their nation once the threat from afar was positive and recognizable.

Kitchener's Armies acquired a new status in the minds of civilians. Before 1914 there was a great social stigma attached to service in the army. The men of the Pals' Battalions, however, were treated with respect and army life became more alluring to men who led dull, anonymous lives. To join up was now looked upon as being the noble thing to do for one's country. Kitchener's appeal was taken up by men of all classes, and in a short time the social base of the army's make-up was transformed.

Never in British history had there been an army with so many of its units directly linked to local areas. The Hull Daily Mail and many other publications churned out an unrelenting barrage of recruiting propaganda, at times reaching hysterical proportions. As time went on it became harder and harder for a man to stand back as his friends and work-mates went off to train for the front.

The first Pals' unit to be raised in Hull was the Commercials, so called because the majority of them came from the commercial classes, were teachers or were employed in other such middle-class occupations. As Ernest Land called them: "They was the nobs battalion and use to snob you a bit". [1] Many of these men were later to hold commissions. The other three Pals' units were made up of working men, many of whom came from backgrounds of great poverty. For every 1,000 births in working-class homes in Hull, 124 died in infancy [2] of diseases that are now eradicated. Housing for the working-classes was spartan, usually a one-up and one-down with no bath and an outside cold-water tap and toilet. Robert Harris Weasenham was raised on Hedon Road and remembered well how, as a boy, he and his play-mates would run barefoot through the streets even in the winter months. He and his wife, Olive, often spoke of their hunger when work was scarce for their fathers and of the harsh discipline in the home. Olive's father had a whip hung at the fireside which he used often on her brother Ernest. [3]

Albert Barker was in service before the war and had to work very long hours for a meagre wage. He was around when the Wolds Waggoners' Reserve was raised at Sledmere and commented on them: "They used to hire them out to anybody, no better than slaves." [4] Ernest Land worked on the land and would have to start work at 4 a.m. to begin a day of hard labour and finish late with no thought of extra pay. [5] These simple men held their tongues and accepted their lot. Life was hard if a man worked but it was much harder if a man did not, especially if he had a family. Olive Weasenham spoke of the fear all working people had of the workhouse on Beverley Road and how families would take children in to their own homes sooner than let them end up there. [6] Taking this grinding poverty into account, there was little wonder many joined up for a change and for some excitement.

As events gathered momentum in August, 1914, and the German army made its victorious advance towards Mons, many thought it was going to be a short conflict that would end with Germany being taught a swift lesson. After the battle of Mons and Le-Cateau the old regular forces of the B.E.F. were decimated after fighting fierce rear-guard actions followed by long retreats in hot humid weather. The news of the true situation began to filter back to Hull and in September recruiting in the city gained momentum.

All the main political parties, city dignitaries and church organizations threw their weight behind the recruiting drive that was given extra strength by the innovation of the new class-based Battalions later known as the 'Pals'. In the Hull Daily Mail photographs of September, 1914, the young men who stepped forward into the ranks of the Hull Pals can still be seen. These images of that time show the enthusiasm felt by the citizens of Hull as they cheered and encouraged Kitchener's men as they marched through the streets. They joined the army to defend their country and the British way of life, even though none of them had any idea of what real warfare was like between industrialized nations.

More than seventy years after the Great War ended it is hard to estimate the way in which individual soldiers regarded their war experience. The non-combatant newspapermen wrote nonsense for the most part, and the majority of soldiers did not leave a written record. The bulk of diaries left come from the men of the Hull Commercials as they were in general men of a higher educational standard, being made up of teachers and clerks. Even diaries left by men from the other three Pals units are, for the most part, from skilled or semi-skilled individuals and are very well written, speaking in great detail of physical and emotional experiences.

Ernest Land, Albert Barker and Robert Harris Weasenham were men of humble origins and spoke of their experiences of war with a mixture of pride, fond memories and sadness. Talking to these men and reading the diaries others left behind conjured up ghosts from that grim time and brought their vivid recollections to life, an experience that was both fascinating and disturbing. Their judgements were at times partial and prejudiced but it is better to represent them as they were; to do otherwise would only distort the meaning of what they went through.

The training of the Hull Battalions and their experience in Egypt was a pleasant jaunt compared to what awaited them in France. The great arsenal of weapons that constantly pummelled the infantrymen became a part of their everyday life in and out of the line. The horrors and deprivations suffered by the front-line men fused units together and formed bonds that were never to be broken unless by death. The memory of those times is as strong in the old men today as it ever was. Gerald Denis admits that he has trouble remembering events from a week ago but can recall his war experience as though it were yesterday, though he would like to forget some things that happened so long in the past.

Talking to the survivors and reading the written records left to us, the most lasting impression that comes across is that of mutual loyalty and good-nature. If these men were ordered to advance they would move forward into the heaviest barrage and machine-gun fire, no matter how intense. When ordered to hold a position they would stand fast until told to retire, overwhelmed or killed. The majority were sociable beings with the ability to be generous and unselfishly courageous in battle, often risking their lives for pals and at times giving their lives for each other.

Under fire they had the capacity to withstand lengthy bombardments of gigantic proportions, an exposure that seems to us today unendurable. All of this they suffered for four long years in a world that was dangerous beyond our comprehension. When at home among civilians who asked about the front they had little to say:

> "No they couldn't understand, I dare not tell them, the people at home couldn't begin to understand." [8]

Elsie Swift of Bean Street, Hull, had three brothers in the Hull Pals and recalled in 1989 how they would come home on leave at various times; she was 12 years old at the time. When asked if they ever spoke of the front to the family she answered without hesitation:

> "Never, never, no they never told you anything." [9]

Words could never convey to non-combatants what it was like to be on the receiving end of barrage or describe the sight of human beings being torn apart before one's eyes and how men choked and squirmed when caught unprepared by a gas attack. Many thousands met their deaths, not gloriously while rushing enemy positions, but in the corner of some squalid muddy trench. This reality existed only at the front and the only others that understood these things were their pals who shared this hard life and whose company made it all bearable. When they had come to the last extremity of hope, when they prepared to go over the top and martyrdoms were inevitable, they only had each other to rely on. This was to form a strong camaderie that was felt by all front-line men and was to be one of the outstanding features of the Great War.

The men of the Hull Pals took the pressures, each man standing at his post while his pals did the same. Not once did they revolt against orders, even though at times the futility of it all was obvious. No Battalion broke into mutiny even when ordered to advance into what seemed like certain death. At Oppy Robert Harris Weasenham felt depressed before the attack but never hesitated to move forward into a hail of machine-gun fire with his mates. The despair of the individual soldier was at times profound but the mass moved as it was directed, from one killing-ground to another. Complaints were frequent and very often justified but when ordered to move against the enemy there was never any hesitation or questioning. Ernest Land commented of the 2nd Hull Pals:

"They were a bloody grand lot o' lads." [10]

And they were.

The end of the Great War came as swiftly as it started. In the early hours of 11th November, 1918, a fierce barrage raged near the positions of the two remaining Hull units, then as 11 a.m. came round a strange silence fell over the entire front and it was over at last. This abrupt finish to the war was felt by the Hull men, who were still in the front line at this time, to be a great anti-climax. The indifference with which the news of the Armistice was received was general among front-line troops. No more need they fear being strafed by Gerry, they could now stand up without the fear of instant death and what had been their sole purpose in life for four years, killing Germans, was ended at a stroke. This was a time of great bewilderment as to what the future now held.

This total lack of elation can be understood if we look at the situation in early November, 1918. In the German offensives of that same year, when the stalemate of the trenches was broken, the Allies had been forced to retreat and in doing so had lost over a third of a million men. Then, as the tide of battle turned, the German army was forced to retire over all its hard-won gains. It looked at this time as though defeat for Germany was only a matter of time as the enemy was pushed back toward the Fatherland. The victories being won in countless actions in the second half of 1918 by the Allies were not to be taken to a logical conclusion and the Germany army was never dissolved. They marched back to Germany intact as a fighting force bearing their arms. The problem of Prussian militarism was not curbed, only dented. This, combined with the political and social unrest in the country, led to a far more terrible conflict twenty years on.

Another reason why men were apprehensive when peace was declared was that they had known only war for most of their adult life and after four years it would mean leaving the vast organization that they had become a part of. Osborne and Pearson both expressed concern about having to enter upon the responsibilities of civilian life. The army had clothed them, fed them and taken care of the bills. As civilians these worries would fall on their own shoulders. It seemed impossible that the vast military machine that they had become so used to would ever release its hold on them.

The front-line troops had been totally involved in the war; death and injury being ever-present affected their mental outlook greatly. Men who had set up mental blocks to the violent world they lived in as a defence against the most dreadful possibilities and had kept at bay the last enemy — death — suddenly found the need for all of this removed. As Pearson remarks, men were tired and sceptical as the war had gone on too long, and this lack of enthusiasm was typical of the soldiers at the front on Armistice Day.

As army discipline eased, no mutinies ensued among the front-line troops of the 'Hull Pals'. Only men frustrated at the slow rate of demobilization revolted at Calais and other areas and these disputes were soon settled. Until demobilization the men waited in France where they were entertained by concerts and games. Schools were set up and they began to prepare for their return to civilian life. As 1918 drew to a close the men awaiting demobilization and those already back in England still had to survive the influenza epidemic wreaking havoc among the population. Pte. Beeston of the Commercials was laid low by the 'flu and felt himself very lucky to live through it:

> "It was bad late in 1918 in our hospital ward in Leeds, many passing on. Come to think of it, surviving two (enemy) attacks in France and then the flu. For the third time in 1918 I came very close to joining the angels prematurely." [11]

Once back home, men were nervy and unsettled. Lewis Osborne spoke of "the old nightmares" and of his restlessness. Robert Weasenham would jump each time he heard a loud bang and it took some time for them to get back into the civilian way of life. Weasenham and Pearson spoke with bitterness of Lloyd George's 'land fit for heroes' and found only unemployment as they returned to a world greatly changed from the one they knew. The past had to be shed and this would take time for the returning soldiers. The civilians were glad to see the war over and although censorship had deprived them of news, the interminable lists of dead could not be ignored. They can still be seen in the Hull Daily Mail, line upon line of them, photographs of young beardless faces not yet marked by adulthood. The sheer numbers of them still have the ability to numb the mind as anyone who wishes to see goes through the hundreds of pages.

Olive Weasenham remembers her brother Ernest being killed at Passchendaele in 1917 and the traumatic effect it had on her mother:

> "She was struck dumb and dressed in black for many weeks after. The curtains in the house were never open and she would sit in darkness, never being the same again." [12]

Their little house in Nornabell Street was never to return to normality again and Olive always blamed her mother's early death on the news of her son's fate.

There were 1,947 men killed serving with the 92nd (Hull) Brigade or 'Hull Pals'. [13] The effects on the loved ones and relatives in Hull were devastating. Individuals and groups of individuals once present in the lives of the bereaved were present no longer. Whole streets had seen their young men wiped out in the great offensives of 1916 and 1917. A street as small as Sharp Street has dozens of names on its roll of honour and it can still be seen today, though the soldiers on it are long since forgotten. The stress of bereavement on the living and the lives cut short can never be measured in numbers of dead and wounded. The heartache felt by that generation and their children was apparent enough at the time and people that experienced it feel it just as keenly

*Many churches in Hull erected their own memorials to the Dead
of the Great War, either in the church or in its grounds.*

*In the churchyard of St Mary's Church in Sculcoates Lane stands a
life-size Crucified Crist, carved from solid wood. Inside the church,
one column is inscribed on three sides with the names of the dead.
A page in the Book of Remembrance is turned each day, and a
prayer said for those whose names appear on the open page.*

*Pte. McColl, who was executed on 28th December, 1917, lived in this parish,
but his name is not recorded here.*

now as they every did. Ask any survivor, civilian or serviceman, about the loss of friends or loved ones in the Great War and their recall is instant and moving in its intensity so long after the event.

The handful of veterans that remain are now well into their nineties. It has been a long time since there has been a reunion of any of the 'Hull Pals' units and the passing of time has taken more than the Germans ever could. The remaining few have become isolated as silent witnesses to a momentous event that is little known except by a few enthusiasts. With the passing of time these men have seen the major happening of their youth, once known as the Great War, become just another distant conflict in the minds of the majority of the population.

But the human witnesses still left can remember vividly the old names: Oppy, Colincamps, Serre, Arras, Fresnoy and the rest. They roll off the tongue as easily as street names in Hull. In their minds the fallen will never age and will continue to haunt their thoughts and dreams until the last survivor succumbs to the inevitable fate of us all. The bayonet men who fought with unflinching devotion at Serre in 1916, at Oppy in 1917, who faced and withstood the German onslaught in early 1918 and defeated the German Army in the field are long since forgotten in Hull. The young of today view the remaining rolls of honour with uncomprehending eyes and the vast numbers of names on these monuments mean little to them.

Statistics of soldiers killed mean nothing to the reader. Only when one visits the cemeteries near the various battlefields do they begin to register. Rank upon rank of pale headstones standing mute in the ground bear witness to the sufferings of these fine young men. The sad beauty of these well-kept places has the ability to move even the coldest heart. The men who lost their lives serving with the 'Hull Pals' are still there:

> Pte. 13/1312. J. H. Swift aged 19 years (K.I.A [14] 13.11.16)
> Pte. 12/903 G. W. Tarling aged 40 years (K.I.A 13.11.16)
> L/Cpl. 10/836 G. L. Spring aged 22 years (K.I.A. 3.5.17)
> L/Sgt. 11/1140 J. R. Haldenby, 30 years (K.I.A. 13.11.16)
> Pte. 13/182 F. W. Midforth aged 23 years (K.I.A 13.11.16) [15]

and all the rest lie in the ground they once fought over.

Inscriptions were carved on many headstones after the war by relatives that visited the cemeteries in the 1920's. Many of them still echo the then official attitudes toward the war:

> "I fell but yielded not my English soul, that lives out here beneath the battle's roll." [16]

Others are more personal and moving in their simplicity giving us a brief glimpse into the grief of the bereaved:

> "Ever in thought dear son." [17]

> "Oh for the touch of a vanished hand, the sound of a voice that is still." [18]

Oppy Village in 1989

Oppy Wood from Baileul, 1989. The wood is still closed to the public as so much live ammunition remains.

Albert Barker was wounded and taken prisoner at Serre on 13th November, 1916. Here he contemplates the grave of his brother Alfred, who died of wounds on 6th August, 1916, while serving with the Hull Commercials.

The battlefields of Serre and Oppy have now been restored, though the hardware of war continues to be found each year. Oppy Wood is still not open to the public as there is so much live ammunition still buried there. The places are now evocative in their silence and as one stands in the battle-zone, it is not hard to imagine those ghosts from so long ago going about their grim business.

The ordinary front-line soldiers of the 'Hull Pals' were not an outstanding section of society and they were not supermen. Ill-used they definitely were, but when their country called they came forward to its defence and played their part. All the diaries and all the men interviewed speak as one when they look back. They were proud to say they had been there and had experienced the camaderie of the trenches. Their experience has now passed into history and with the death of the last survivor will go a part of the life of Hull and a generation the like of which we shall not see again.

NOTES

1. Land, E. Pte. 11/648. 11th East Yorkshires, 1914-1918. Taped interview, 1989 (Author's collection).
2. Becket, F. W. and Simpson, K. A Nation in Arms. (Manchester University Press, 1985). p.203.
3. Weasenham, R. H. and O. B. Conversations with author, early 1960's.
4. Barker, A. L/Cpl. 13th East Yorkshires, 1914-1918. Taped interview, 1988 (Author's collection).
5. Land, E. Pte. 11th East Yorkshires, 1914-1918. Taped interview, 1989 (Author's collection).
6. Now the Kingston General Hospital, Beverley Road, Hull.
7. Denis, G. K.R.R.C. 1915-1918. Taped interview, 1988. (Author's collection).
8. Ibid.
9. Bancroft (Formerly Swift) E. Mrs. Taped interview, 1989. (Author's collection).
10. Land, E. Pte. 11/648. 11th East Yorkshires, 1914-1918. Taped interview, 1989. (Author's collection).
11. Beeston, F. Hull Commercials. Letter to author, 1989.
12. Weasenham, O. Conversation with author, 1960's.
13. Soliders Died in the Great War. (Maywood & Son, 1989.) pp.57-75.
14. K.I.A. — Killed in action.
15. The following relatives of the soldiers mentioned have contacted me concerning my study:
Mrs. Elsie Bancroft, now living in Hull. Sister of J. H. Swift.
Mrs. Lily Millington, now living in Hull. Niece of G. W. Tarling.
Mr. J. Leighton, now living in Gilberdyke. His mother-in-law was the niece of J. R. Haldenby.
Mr. Arthur Lewis Palethorpe, now living in Hull. Great nephew of G. L. Spring.
Mrs. A. Allen, now living in Hull. Niece of F. W. Midforth.
16. Inscription on the grave of Sgt. 12/525. J. W. Streets (Age 31) K.I.A. 1.7.16.
17. Inscription on the grave of Pte. 10/525. W. E. Adamson (Age 21) Died of wounds, 2.7.16.
18. Inscription on the grave of Pte. 10/507. J. A. Dobbs M.M. (Age 21) K.I.A. 2.9.16.

APPENDIX I

Victoria Cross Awards (Hull Pals)

CITATIONS PUBLISHED IN THE LONDON GAZETTE, 1917

No. 12/21 Pte. JOHN CUNNINGHAM, 12th (S.) Bn. East Yorkshire Regiment

Opposite Hebuterne Sector, France, 13th November, 1916

For most conspicuous bravery and resource during operations

After the enemy's front line had been captured, Pte. Cunningham proceeded with a bombing section up a communication trench. Much opposition was encountered, and the rest of the section became casualties. Collecting all the bombs from the casualties, this gallant soldier went on alone. Having expended all his bombs, he returned for a fresh supply and again proceeded to the communication trench, where he met a party of ten of the enemy. These he killed and cleared the trench up to the enemy line.

His conduct throughout the day was magnificent.

(L.G. No. 29901, 13/1/17)

T/2nd LIEUT. JOHN HARRISON, M.C., 11th (S.) Bn. East Yorkshire Regiment

Oppy, France, 3rd May, 1917

For most conspicuous bravery and self-sacrifice in an attack

Owing to darkness and to smoke from the enemy barrage, and from our own, and to the fact that our objective was in a dark wood, it was impossible to see when our barrage had lifted off the enemy front line.

Nevertheless, 2nd Lieut. Harrison led his company against the enemy trench under heavy rifle and machine-gun fire, but was repulsed. Re-organising his command as best he could in No Man's Land, he again attacked in darkness under terrific fire, but with no success.

Then, turning round, this gallant officer single-handed made a dash at the machine gun, hoping to knock out the gun and so save the lives of many of his company.

His self-sacrifice and absolute disregard of danger was an inspiring example to us all. (He is reported missing, believed killed.)

(L.G. No. 30130, 14th June, 1917)

APPENDIX II

WAR GRAVES

10th, 11th, 12th and 13th Battalions, East Yorkshire Regiment (Hull Pals).

Some of these men were not in the Hull Pals Units when they died but their numbers show the Battalion they enlisted in. Men enlisting early in the war would have the number of their Battalion before the Regimental number, i.e. 11/682 would be an 11th Battalion man who was the 682nd to enlist when it was formed. Others of the Hull Pals without this type of number would have been drafted in later in the war, often from other Regiments.

HULL (HEDON ROAD) CEMETERY)

BROOKS, Pte. C.H., 13/949, 'A' Company, 13th Battalion, East Yorkshire Regiment. Died of wounds (Gas), 6th May, 1918, age 36. Son of Thomas and Ellen Brooks of Grimsby; Husband of the late Selina Brooks. 153. 8.

BROWN, Pte. Adrian, 13/44, East Yorkshire Regiment, 5th March, 1919. Age 30. Husband of Emma Brown of 2 Scarborough Terrace, Barnsley Street, Holderness Road, Hull. 135. 90.

BROWN, Pte. John Henry, 12/328. Depot, East Yorkshire Regiment. Died of tuberculosis, 19th January, 1920, age 29. Son of William James and Mary Elizabeth Brown of 2 Railway Cottages, Sutton Bank, Dansom Lane, Hull. 378. 72.

BURR, Pte. James, 13/847. 13th Battalion, East Yorkshire Regiment. Transferred to (605926) 42nd Prisoner of War Company Labour Corps. 7th May, 1919. Husband of Mrs. Booth (formerly Burr) of 15 Georges Terrace, Hert Street, Hull. 377. 1.

BUTLER, Pte. A.C., 11/263. Depot Battalion, East Yorkshire Regiment. 31st July, 1916. Husband of A. E. Butler of 59 Woodhouse Street, Hedon Road, Hull. 307. 95.

COLLINGWOOD, Pte. Joseph William, 10/338. Depot, East Yorkshire Regiment. Died of wounds, 11th July, 1918, age 21. Son of Joseph and Margaret Collingwood of 536 Holderness Road, Hull. 368. 75.

FISHER, Pte. Charles Herbert, 11/57. 11th Battalion, East Yorkshire Regiment. Transferred to (416904) Labour Corps. 29th August, 1919. Age 38. Husband of Harriet Fisher of 2 Sophia's Place, Percy Street, Hull. 376. 7.

MANN, Pte, John, 13/1148. Depot, East Yorkshire Regiment. Died of pneumonia following wounds, 16th November, 1918, age 26. Son of James and Sarah Mann of 97 Arundel Street, Holderness Road, Hull. Enlisted December, 1914, served in Egypt and France. 374. 68.

PADGET, Pte, Charles, 368, 'D' Company, 13th Battalion, East Yorkshire Regiment. Died of phthisis, 23rd August, 1921. Son of Hannah Mary Padget of 31 Brook Street, Hull and the late John Padget. 252. 34.

SOWERBY, Pte. F., 12/1044. 12th Battalion, East Yorkshire Regiment. 25th November, 1916, age 39. Son of Alison Sowerby of Hull. Husband of Mary Ann Sowerby of 3 Sarah Ann's Terrace, Spyvee Street, Hull. 249. 34.

TAYLOR, Pte. Henry Wright, 12/894. Depot, East Yorkshire Regiment. 25th March, 1919, age 37. Son of William and Mary Taylor of 14 Lime Terrace, Crowle Street, Hedon Road, Hull. Native of Walkington, Beverley, Yorkshire. 342. 8.

WARD, Pte. F., 11/428. 11th Battalion, East Yorkshire Regiment. Died of pneumonia, 16th June, 1915. 87 Eton Street, Hull. 78. 30.

HULL WESTERN CEMETERY, SPRING BANK

BENTLEY, Pte. Harold, 11/1141. 11th Battalion, East Yorkshire Regiment. Died of wounds, 28th April, 1918, age 23. Son of Robert and Amanda Bentley, 50 Sharp Street, Newland Avenue, Hull. 62. 6201.

BENTLEY, Pte. R., 11/1435. 11th Battalion, East Yorkshire Regiment. Died of pneumonia, 5th December, 1918, age 27. Son of Robert and Amanda Bentley, 50 Sharp Street, Newland Avenue, Hull. 62. 6201.

BODFIELD, Pte. Albert Edward, 13/677. 13th Battalion, East Yorkshire Regiment. 25th February, 1915, age 36. Son of the late William and Mary Bodfield of Hull. Husband of Susannah Bodfield of 24 Oxford Street, Scarborough. 535. 51609.

CROOKES, C. S. M. Herbert Clifford, 13/32. 'D' Company, 7th Battalion, East Yorkshire Regiment. Mentioned in dispatches, died of wounds (Gas) 30th March, 1919, age 35. Son of Joseph and Elizabeth Crookes of Hull; husband of Aida Crookes of 12 Kimberley Street, Argyle Street, Hull. 52. 50354.

DAVIE, 2nd Lt. Frank M.M. 11th Battalion, East Yorkshire Regiment. Died of wounds, 2nd June, 1917, age 26. Son of John and Louisa Davie, 62 Sunny Bank, Hull. 216. 21037.

DEWS, Pte. Percy William, 25167. 12th Battalion, East Yorkshire Regiment. 11th February, 1918, age 27. Son of Emma Elizabeth Hepworth of 84 Eton Street, Hessle Road, Hull. 518. 50012.

EDMOND, Pte. S., 11/1328. 11th Battalion, East Yorkshire Regiment. 4th August, 1919. 26. 2466.

FISHER, Pte. Fred, 1249. 13th Battalion, East Yorkshire Regiment. Died of wounds (Gas) 25th January, 1921, age 25. Son of the late Thomas and Elizabeth Fisher. 521. 50298.

GILL, Pte, Thomas, 12/862. 'C' Company, 12th Battalion, East Yorkshire Regiment. 3rd November, 1914, age 24. Son of Annie Gill and the late Thomas Gill; Husband of Mabel Rapson (formerly Gill) of 2 Lillian's Terrace, Woodhouse Street, Hedon Road, Hull. 99. 9804.

HALL, Pte. A., 12/747. 12th Battalion, East Yorkshire Regiment. 5th February, 1915. 418. 40351.

HARDING, Pte. William Walter. 12/2. 12th Battalion, East Yorkshire Regiment, 10th June, 1916, age 28. Son of the late W. Harding and of M. Neale (formerly Harding. 538. 51926.

HASNIP, Sgt. Clifford Channer, 13/346. 'B' Company, 13th Battalion, East Yorkshire Regiment, 12th February, 1919, age 39. Son of James Edward and Ann Sophia Hasnip of Hull; Husband of Florence Hasnip, 13 Wyndham Street, Hull. 346. 33441.

HAWCROFT, Pte. Harry, 12/377. 12th Battalion, East Yorkshire Regiment. 18th December, 1916, age 33. 457. 44127.

HOLMES, Pte. Frank Harold, 12/1364. 12th Battalion, East Yorkshire Regiment. 6th March, 1919, age 33. Son of Henry and Annie Elizabeth Holmes; Husband of Beatrice Gertrude Holmes of 9 Malvern Terrace, Gillet Street, Hessle Road, Hull. 539. 52013.

JOHNSON, Pte. Arthur, 12/1124. 12th Battalion, East Yorkshire Regiment. 19th July, 1918, age 29. Husband of Violet Gertrude Johnson of 12 Victoria Terrace, Beeton Street, Holderness Road, Hull. 551. 53163.

KING, Pte. W., 12/745. 12th Battalion, East Yorkshire Regiment. 12th July, 1916. Step brother of Mrs. A. Watson of 2 Adelaide Street, Scott Street, Hull. 542. 52296.

LAUGHTON, Pte. F. 13/1211. 13th Battalion, East Yorkshire Regiment. 2nd July, 1918. Husband of A. Laughton of 5 Norfolk Place, Norfolk Street, Hull. 327. 31634.

LITTLE, Pte. Joseph Henry, 551175. 10th Battalion, East Yorkshire Regiment. Died of wounds, 26th October, 1918. Son of Mr. H. C. and Mrs. F. Little of 90 Plane Street, Hull. 217. 21109.

MEE, Pte. G., 12/573. 12th Battalion, East Yorkshire Regiment. 13th April, 1921, age 32. Brother-in-law of Mrs. Kate Grundy of 60 Rugby Street, Hessle Road, Hull. 486. 46941.

NEEDHAM, Pte. Patrick, 31010. 11th Battalion, East Yorkshire Regiment. 13th March, 1921, age 46. Son of John and Bridge Needham of Liverpool; Husband of Blanche Edna Needham of 15 Goodwin Terrace, Day Street, Hull. 380. 36764.

REDMORE, L/CPl. H. Harold, 10/544. 14th Battalion, East Yorkshire Regiment. 13th September, 1916, age 25. Son of Edward King Redmore and Catherine Redmore of Hull; Husband of Minnie Ida Redmore of 7 Glencoe Avenue, Flinton Street, Hull. 529. 51032.

ROGERS, Pte. Joseph William, 12/1429. 12th Battalion, East Yorkshire Regiment. Died of heart failure, 23rd October, 1918, age 37. Husband of the late Helen Ryan (Formerly Rogers). 511. 49296.

SMITH, Pte. G., 12/1235. 3rd Battalion, East Yorkshire Regiment. 7th December, 1918. Husband of Mrs. B. B. W. Smith of Nelson Terrace, Bean Street, Hessle Road, Hull. 552. 53280.

SMITH, R.Q.M.S., R., 11/589. 3rd Battalion, East Yorkshire Regiment. 28th April, 1918. Husband of M. E. Smith of Hull. 480. 46392.

SMITH, Pte. Thomas Arthur, 13/231. 'A' Company, 3rd Battalion, East Yorkshire Regiment. Died of cerebral haemorrhage, 31st October, 1918, age 35. Husband of Fanny Elizabeth Smith of 5 William's Terrace, Walcott Street, Hessle Road, Hull. 543. 52435.

TAYLOR, L/Cpl. A.W., 10/17. 10th Battalion, East Yorkshire Regiment. 6th August, 1916. Husband of Mrs. B.A. Taylor of 112 Regent Street, Anlaby Road, Hull. 271. 26305.

TODD, Pte. Harry Rupert, 10/859. 10th Battalion, East Yorkshire Regiment. Died of wounds 14th January, 1917, age 25. Son of the late William Henry and Mary Ann Todd of Barton-on-Humber, Lincolnshire. 473. 45606.

TOMKINS, Pte. Ernest, 25092. 13th Battalion, East Yorkshire Regiment. Died of wounds 16th June, 1917, age 38. Son of Arthur and Charlotte Tomkins of Bayston, Salop. Husband of Selina Tomkins of 3 Sutton Street, Spring Bank, Hull. 17. 1591.

WILLIAMSON, Pte. G.F. 14/172. 10th Battalion, East Yorkshire Regiment. 26th November, 1916. Son of Mrs. E. J. Williamson of 31 St. Andrew's Street, Hessle Road, Hull. 535. 51650.

HULL NORTHERN CEMETERY (COTTINGHAM ROAD)

CRACROFT, Pte. Thomas Richard, 11/1374. 11th Battalion, East Yorkshire Regiment, 26th August, 1921, age 40. Son of John James and Catherine Cracroft of 68 Symonds Street, Fountain Road, Hull. 87. 66.

CRAYTON, Pte. Tom Harold, 10/1124. 'D' Company, 10th Battalion, East Yorkshire Regiment, 11th March, 1918, age 33. Son of the late Richard and Elizabeth Crayton of Nottingham. 41. 9.

EARLE, Pte. Albert Henry, 13/1449. 8th Battalion, East Yorkshire Regiment. Died of wounds, 27th June, 1917, age 19. Son of Henry and Mary Frances Earle of 32 Farringdon Street, Stepney Lane, Hull. 40. 10.

GUEST, Sgt. J., 10/632. Depot, East Yorkshire Regiment, 17th February, 1919, age 30. Husband of Florence Guest of 25 Falmouth Street, Hull. 41. 63.

JUDE, L/Cpl. M.V., 10/1448. Depot, East Yorkshire Regiment, 15th December, 1916. 39. 88.

MILLER, C.Q.M.S. Charles William, 11/926. 4th (Reserve) Battalion, East Yorkshire Regiment. Mentioned in dispatches, 26th August, 1918, age 40. Husband of G. E. Miller of 91 Chanterlands Avenue, Hull. 62. 58.

VAREY, Pte. Walter Ernest, 203055. 10th Battalion, East Yorkshire Regiment. Died of wounds (Gas), 20th December, 1920 age 26. Son of Mr. and Mrs. Arthur Varey of 150 Sharp Street, Newland Avenue, Hull; husband of Cissie Varey of North Cave, Brough, Yorkshire. 107. 57.

WILLEY, Pte. George, 39673. 'D' Company, 10th Battalion, East Yorkshire Regiment. Died of wounds, 4th January, 1919, age 39. Husband of Elizabeth Francis Willey of 23 Bromley Street, Hull. 38. 64.

HULL (HOLY TRINITY, HESSLE ROAD) CEMETERY
DIVISION ROAD, HULL.

BAKER, Pte. Charles Wilford, 13/897. 'C' Company, 13th Battalion, East Yorkshire Regiment. Died of sickness, 6th March, 1915, age 24. Son of Charles Baker of Hull; husband of Ruth Esther Miller (formerly Baker) of 49 Eton Road, Stockton-on-Tees. D.13. 7724.

BOURNER, Cadet Percey, 10/35. 2nd (Officer Cadet) Battalion, East Yorkshire Regiment, 16th May, 1918, age 24. Son of Mary Bourner of 20 Chestnut Grove, Park Road, Hull and the late David Edward Bourner. B.6. 8006.

GRIMMER, Pte. R. J. G., 11/777. 11th Battalion, East Yorkshire Regiment. 17th September, 1916, age 38. Son of James Walter and Tresa Adline Martha Grimmer of 95 Rosamund Street, Hessle Road, Hull. B.4. 7862.

SCULCOATES (SACRISTY) CEMETERY, SCULCOATES LANE
(It is divided by the road into the old and new Grounds)

HEDGES, Pte. Noel Victor, 20248. 10th Battalion, East Yorkshire Regiment. Died of wounds, 8th July, 1916, age 20. Son of John and Kate Hedges of Hull. (Old ground).

APPENDIX III

The Schlieffen Plan

(GERMAN PLAN OF BATTLE — 1914)

The Germans were faced with the problem that the combined forces of themselves and Austria were decidedly inferior to those of France and Russia. To offset this adverse balance, however, they had a central position and the anticipation that Russia's mobilization would be too slow to allow her to exert serious pressure in the opening weeks. While this assumption might suggest a decisive blow at Russia before she was ready, it was equally probable that she would concentrate her main forces too far back for such a German blow to reach — and the experience of Napoleon was not an example to encourage an advance deep into the interior of Russia, with its vast distances and poor communications. The plan long since adopted by Germany was, therefore, to deliver a rapid offensive against France while holding the Russian advanced forces at bay; and later, when France was crushed, to deal with the Russian army. But this plan, in turn, was complicated by the great natural and artificial barriers which the French frontier offered to an invader. It was narrow, only some 150 miles across, and so afforded little room to manoeuvre or even to deploy the masses that Germany planned to launch against her foe. At the south-eastern end it abutted on Switzerland, and after a short stretch of flat country known as the Gap of Belfort the frontier ran for seventy miles along the Vosges mountains. Behind and prolonging this natural rampart ran an almost continuous fortress system, based on Epinal, Toul, Verdun, and twenty miles beyond the last-named lay not only the frontiers of Luxembourg and Belgium but the difficult Ardennes country. Apart from the strongly defended avenues of advance by Belfort and Verdun, the only feasible gap in this barrier was the Trouée de Charmes between Epinal and Toul, left open originally as a strategic trap in which the Germans could be first caught and then crushed by a French counterstroke.

Faced with such a mental and physical blank wall, the logical military course was to go round it — by a wide manoeuvre through Belgium. Graf Schlieffen, Chief of the German General Staff from 1890 to 1905, conceived and developed the plan, by which the French armies were to be enveloped and a rapid decision gained; and as finally formulated it came into force in 1905. To attain its object Schlieffen's plan concentrated the mass of the German forces on the right wing for a gigantic wheel and designedly took risks by reducing the left wing, facing the French frontier, to the slenderest possible size. The swinging mass, pivoting on the fortified area Metz-Thionville, was to consist of fifty-three divisions, backed up as rapidly as possible by Landwehr and Ersatz formations, while the secondary army on the left wing comprised only eight divisions. Its very weakness promised to aid the main blow in a further way, for if a French offensive pressed the left wing back towards the Rhine, the attack through Belgium on the French flank would be all the more difficult to parry.It would be like a revolving door — if a man pressed heavily on one side the other side would swing round and strike him in the back. Here lay the real subtlety of the plan, not in the mere geographical detour.

BIBLIOGRAPHY

ALLISON, W. and FAIRLEY, J. The Monocled Mutineer. (Quartet, 1986)

ASCOLI, D. The Mons Star. (Harrap, 1984)

BABBINGTON, A. For the Sake of Example. (Leo Cooper, 1984)

BARKER, A.J. The East Yorkshire Regiment. (Leo Cooper, 1971)

BECKET, I. F. W. and SIMPSON, K. A Nation in Arms. (Manchester University Press, 1985)

BRITTAIN, V. Testament of Youth. (Fontana, 1980)

BURGOYNE, G. A. The Burgoyne Diaries. (Harmsworth, 1985)

CARVER, R. B., FENWICK, J. M., GRAYSTONE, J. W., PAGE, F. G. and THIRSK, G. W. A History of the 10th (Service) Battalion, East Yorkshire Regiment, 1914-1919. (Brown and Sons, 1937)

CASSER, G. H. Kitchener. (William Kimber, 1977)

DESAGNEAUX, H. A French Soldier's War Diary, 1914-1918. (Elmfield Press, 1975)

DOLDEN, A. S. Cannon Fodder. (Blandford, 1980)

FARRAR, P. Hull's New Army, 1914. Journal of Local Studies, Vol. 1, No. 2, Spring 1981.

FUSSEL, P. The Great War and Modern Memory. (Oxford, 1977)

GERMAINS, V. W. The Kitchener Armies. (Peter Davies, 1930)

GEORGE, D. L. War Memoirs of David Lloyd George. (Odhams, 1938)

GRAVES, R. Goodbye to all that. (Penguin, 1986)

HODGES, F. J. Men of 18 in 1918. (A. H. Stockwell Ltd., 1988)

HORNE, A. The Price of Glory, Verdun, 1916. (Penguin, 1982)

KEEGAN, J. The Face of Battle. (Penguin, 1986)

KNIGHTLEY, P. The First Casualty. (Quartet, 1975)

LIDDEL-HART, B. History of the First World War. (Pan Books, 1970)

LONGWORTH, P. The Unending Vigil. (Secker & Warburg, 1985)

MACDONALD, L. Somme. (Macmillan, 1983)

MACDONALD, L. 1914. (Michael Joseph, 1987)

MACDONALD L. They called it Passchendaele. (Macmillan, 1978)

MACDONALD, L. The Roses of No-Man's Land. (Macmillan, 1987)

MANNING, F. The Middle Parts of Fortune. (Buchan-Enright, 1986)

MIDDLEBROOKE, M. The First Day on the Somme. (Penguin, 1984)

PEACOCK, A. J. Gunfire, No. 1. (York Educational Supplement, 1982)

REMARQUE, E.M. All Quiet on the Western Front. (Putnam, 1980)

RICHARDS, I., GOODSON, J. B. and MORRIS, J. A. A Sketchmap History of the Great War and After. (Harrap and Co. Ltd., 1956)

ROTHSTEIN, A. The Soldier's Strikes of 1918. (Macmillan, 1980)

SASSOON, S. Memoirs of an Infantry Officer. (Faber, 1926)

SHEFFIELD, D.G. World War One. (Bison Books, 1987)

SHEPPARD, T. Hull Before, During and After the Great War. (Brown, 1919)

SIMKINS, R. Kitchener's Army. (Manchester University Press, 1988)

SLACK, C. M. Grandfather's Adventures in the Great War, 1914-18. (Stockwell Ltd., 1977)

TAYLOR, A. J. P. The First World War. (Penguin, 1987)

TAYLOR, A. J. P. English History, 1914-1945. (Oxford University Press, 1985)

TERRAINE, J. To Win a War. (Macmillan, 1986)

WATT, W. M. Dare Call it Treason. (Chatto and Windus, 1964)

WEINTRAUB, S. A Stillness Heard Around the World, The End of the Great War, November, 1918. (Allen and Unwin, 1985)

WILSON, T. The Myriad Faces of War. (Blackwell/Polity, 1986)

WINTER, D. Death's Men. (Penguin, 1985)

WINTER, J. M. The Experience of World War One. (Macmillan, 1988)

WOODWARD, D. R. Lloyd George and the Generals. (Associated University Presses, 1983)

WYRRELL, E. The East Yorkshire Regiment in the Great War. (Harrison & Sons Ltd., 1928)

DIARIES

BATES, H. 11th East Yorkshire, 1914 to 1918. (Loaned by his son, William Bates of Cottingham. Copy in author's collection). Unpublished.

BEEKEN, J. L/Cpl. 10/685. Hull Commercials, 1916-1918. (Imperial War Museum. Copy in author's collection). Unpublished.

CARTER, Pte. Hull Commercials, 1916-1918. (Imperial War Museum. Copy in author's collection). Unpublished.

CLAPPISON, R. E. 1300. Hull Commercials, 'C' Company, 1914-1918. (Loaned by his son, Bob Clappison, Hull. Copy in author's collection). Unpublished.

GRAYSTONE, J. W. Pte. 10/634. Hull Commercials, 1914-1918. (Imperial War Museum. Copy in author's collection). Unpublished.

McNALLY, P., R. S. M. 11/1087. 11th East Yorkshire, 1914-1918. (Loaned by his son John McNally of Hull. Copy in author's collection). Unpublished.

OSBORNE, L. S. Pte. 11/341. 11th East Yorkshire, 1914-1918. (Loaned by Mr. McDougal of Hull. Copy in author's collection). Unpublished.

PEARSON, R. Pte. 10/1180. Hull Commercials, 1915-1918. (Loaned by Mr. Godrey Hanwell of Cottingham. Copy in author's collection). Unpublished.

TAIT, J. Pte. 10/1281. Hull Commercials, 1915-1916. (Malet Lambert Local History Originals, Hull. Vol.8, 1982).

THORPE, G. Resident of Hull, August, 1914. (Hull Local History Library). Unpublished.

LETTERS (UNPUBLISHED)

HEBB, C. Pte. 1885. 1/4th East Yorkshires, 1914-1918. (Loaned by Mrs. Pauline Best of Beverley. Copies in author's collection).

SPENCER, S. L/Cpl. 1/4th East Yorkshires, 1918. (Hull Local History Library).

WILLIAMS, E. C. Cpt. Egypt, 1916. (Imperial War Museum. Copies in author's collection).

BEESTON, F. Hull Commercials, 1918. Now living in Ipswich. Letter to the author in 1989.

TAPED INTERVIEWS (Author's Collection)

DENIS, G. ex K.R.R.C. 1915-1918, Now living in Hull, 1989.

LANDS, E. ex 11th East Yorkshires, 1914-1918. Now living in Ellerker, 1989.

BARKER, A. ex 13th East Yorkshire, 1914-1918. Now living in Cottingham, 1989.

SLACK, C. ex 1/4th East Yorkshires. Has since died.

BANCROFT, E. Mrs. Now living in Hull.

RECOLLECTIONS

ROBERT HARRIS WEASENHAM was my grandfather and raised me in Hull. Any quotes referring to him are the results of conversations with him. My grandmother, Olive Bertha Weasenham, quoted in Chapter 3, died February, 1990.

The quote from HENRY WEST, 1/4th East Yorkshires, used in Trials and Tribulations was given to me by his grandson, Mr. Graham Boddy of Cottingham.

MATERIAL FROM THE PUBLIC RECORDS OFFICE, KEW.

Operations carried out by the 31st Division, 13th November, 1916. (WO.95/41). Unpublished.

Reports made by wounded and unwounded officers and men who went into action with the attacking Battalions, 13th November, 1916. (WO. 95/41). Unpublished.

Account of attack, 13th November, 1916. (WO. 95/41). Unpublished.

War Diary, H.Q 92nd Brigade, 13th November, 1916. (95/2356). Unpublished.

Points noted for consideration when undertaking offensive operations in future. Post 13th November, 1916, attack. (95/41). Unpublished.

Secret. 93rd Infantry Brigade Operation order No. 57. 10th November, 1916. (95/2356). Unpublished.

Secret. 92nd Infantry Brigade Instructions, October, 1916. (95/2356). Unpublished.

Copies of all the above are in the author's collection.

OTHER SOURCES

Infantry Training Manual, 1914. (War Office, 1914).

Manual of Military Law, 1914. (War Office, 1914).

Musketry Regulations, Part One, 1909. (War Office, 1909).

Hull Daily News, Peace Edition, 1919. (Copy in author's collection).

The War Graves of the British Empire, Hull. (Imperial War Graves Commission, 1926).

Carmichael, C. Sgt. A Yeoman on the Somme. (Copy in author's collection).

Cpt. Wooley, R. M. (Typed Statement) 'D' Company, 13th East Yorkshires. (Copy in author's collection . 13th November, 1916.

War Diary. 10th, 11th, 12th and 13th Battalions, East Yorkshire Regiment. 1914-1918. (Prince of Wales Own Museum, York).

Soldiers Died in the Great War, Part 20, The East Yorkshire Regiment. (Haywood and Son, 1989).

By Some of Them. A Short Diary of the 11th (S) Battalion, East Yorkshire Regiment, 1914-1919. (Brown and Son, 1921).

Recommendation for Military Cross. 2nd Lt. V. H. Jenkin, 11th Battalion, East Yorkshire Regiment, 11th November, 1917, for gallantry in trench raid, 8th November, 1917. (Imperial War Museum. Copy in author's collection).

The Hull Daily Mail. 1914 to 1918. (Hull Local History Library — Microfilm).

The Hull Times. 1914. (Hull Local History Library — Microfilm).

The Dawn. Hull Labour Publication, 1915. (Hull Local History Library).